ENGLISH
FOR EVERYONE

COURSE BOOK
LEVEL ❶ BEGINNER

FREE AUDIO
website and app
www.dkefe.com

Author

Rachel Harding has a background in English-language teaching and is now a full-time author of English-language learning materials. She has written for major English-language publishers including Oxford University Press.

Course consultant

Tim Bowen has taught English and trained teachers in more than 30 countries worldwide. He is the co-author of works on pronunciation teaching and language-teaching methodology, and author of numerous books for English-language teachers. He is currently a freelance materials writer, editor, and translator. He is a member of the Chartered Institute of Linguists.

Language consultant

Professor Susan Barduhn is an experienced English-language teacher, teacher trainer, and author, who has contributed to numerous publications. In addition to directing English-language courses in at least four different continents, she has been President of the International Association of Teachers of English as a Foreign Language, and an adviser to the British Council and the US State Department. She is currently a Professor at the School for International Training in Vermont, USA.

ENGLISH
FOR EVERYONE

COURSE BOOK

LEVEL 1 BEGINNER

Editors Gareth Clark, Lisa Gillespie, Andrew Kerr-Jarrett
Art Editors Chrissy Barnard, Ray Bryant
Senior Art Editor Sharon Spencer
Editorial Assistants Jessica Cawthra, Sarah Edwards
Illustrators Edwood Burn, Denise Joos, Michael Parkin, Jemma Westing
Audio Producer Liz Hammond
Managing Editor Daniel Mills
Managing Art Editor Anna Hall
Project Manager Christine Stroyan
Jacket Designer Natalie Godwin
Jacket Editor Claire Gell
Jacket Design Development Manager Sophia MTT
Producer, Pre-Production Luca Frassinetti
Producer Mary Slater
Publisher Andrew Macintyre
Art Director Karen Self
Publishing Director Jonathan Metcalf

DK India
Jacket Designer Surabhi Wadhwa
Managing Jackets Editor Saloni Singh
Senior DTP Designer Harish Aggarwal

First published in Great Britain in 2016 by
Dorling Kindersley Limited
80 Strand, London, WC2R 0RL

A CIP catalogue record for this book
is available from the British Library.
ISBN: 978-0-2412-2631-5

Printed and bound in China

All images © Dorling Kindersley Limited
For further information see: www.dkimages.com

A WORLD OF IDEAS:
SEE ALL THERE IS TO KNOW

www.dk.com

Contents

How the course works

English for Everyone is designed for people who want to teach themselves the English language. Like all language courses, it covers the core skills: grammar, vocabulary, pronunciation, listening, speaking, reading, and writing. Unlike in other courses, the skills are taught and practiced as visually as possible, using images and graphics to help you understand and remember. The best way to learn is to work through the book in order, making full use of the audio available on the website and app. Turn to the practice book at the end of each unit to reinforce your learning with additional exercises.

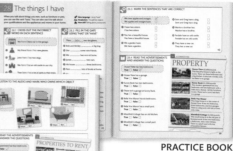

PRACTICE BOOK

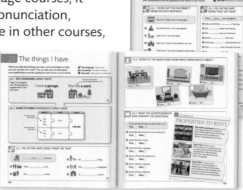

COURSE BOOK

Unit number The book is divided into units. The unit number helps you keep track of your progress.

Learning points Every unit begins with a summary of the key learning points.

Modules Each unit is broken down into modules, which should be done in order. You can take a break from learning after completing any module.

Language learning Modules with colored backgrounds teach new vocabulary and grammar. Study these carefully before moving on to the exercises.

Audio support Most modules have supporting audio recordings of native English speakers to help you improve your speaking and listening skills.

Exercises Modules with white backgrounds contain exercises that help you practice your new skills to reinforce learning.

FREE AUDIO
website and app
www.dkefe.com

Language modules

New language points are taught in carefully graded stages, starting with a simple explanation of when they are used, then offering further examples of common usage, and a detailed breakdown of how key constructions are formed.

Module number Every module is identified with a unique number, so you can track your progress and easily locate any related audio.

Module heading The teaching topic appears here, along with a brief introduction.

Sample language New language points are introduced in context. Colored highlights make new constructions easy to spot, and annotations explain them.

Graphic guide Clear, simple visuals help to explain the meaning of new language forms and when to use them, and also act as an aid to learning and recall.

Supporting audio This symbol indicates that the model sentences featured in the module are available as audio recordings.

Formation guide Visual guides break down English grammar into its simplest parts, showing you how to recreate even complex formations.

Vocabulary Throughout the book, vocabulary modules list the most common and useful English words and phrases, with visual cues to help you remember them.

Write-on lines You are encouraged to write your own translations of English words to create your own reference pages.

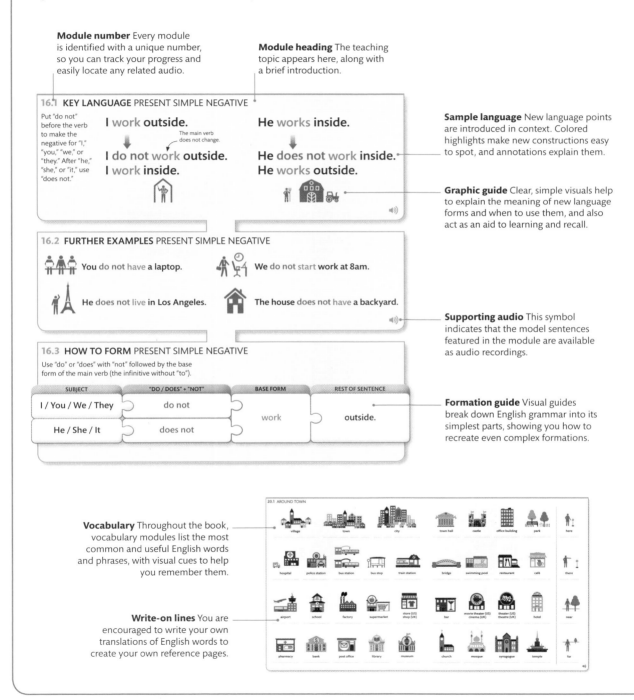

16.1 KEY LANGUAGE PRESENT SIMPLE NEGATIVE

Put "do not" before the verb to make the negative for "I," "you," "we," or "they." After "he," "she," or "it," use "does not."

I work outside.

I do not work outside.
I work inside.

He works inside.

The main verb does not change.

He does not work inside.
He works outside.

16.2 FURTHER EXAMPLES PRESENT SIMPLE NEGATIVE

You do not have a laptop.

We do not start work at 8am.

He does not live in Los Angeles.

The house does not have a backyard.

16.3 HOW TO FORM PRESENT SIMPLE NEGATIVE

Use "do" or "does" with "not" followed by the base form of the main verb (the infinitive without "to").

SUBJECT	"DO / DOES" + "NOT"	BASE FORM	REST OF SENTENCE
I / You / We / They	do not	work	outside.
He / She / It	does not		

20.1 AROUND TOWN

village · town · city · town hall · castle · office building · park · here
hospital · police station · bus station · bus stop · train station · bridge · swimming pool · restaurant · café · there
airport · school · factory · supermarket · store (US) shop (UK) · bar · movie theater (US) cinema (UK) · theater (US) theatre (UK) · hotel · near
pharmacy · bank · post office · library · museum · church · mosque · synagogue · temple · far

Practice modules

Each exercise is carefully graded to drill and test the language taught in the corresponding course book units. Working through the exercises alongside the course book will help you remember what you have learned and become more fluent. Every exercise is introduced with a symbol to indicate which skill is being practiced.

 GRAMMAR Apply new language rules in different contexts.

 READING Examine target language in real-life English contexts.

 LISTENING Test your understanding of spoken English.

 VOCABULARY Cement your understanding of key vocabulary.

 SPEAKING Compare your spoken English to model audio recordings.

Module number Every module is identified with a unique number, so you can easily locate answers and related audio.

Exercise instruction Every exercise is introduced with a brief instruction, telling you what you need to do.

13.10 FILL IN THE GAPS BY PUTTING THE VERBS IN THE CORRECT FORM

He _finishes_ (finish) work at 5 o'clock.

Sample answer The first question of each exercise is answered for you, to help make the task easy to understand.

① Lucia _____ (wake) up at 7am.

② I _____ (get) up at 7:30am.

③ Ethan _____ (go) to work at 5am.

④ You _____ (leave) work at 5pm.

⑤ Shona _____ (watch) TV in the evening.

Space for writing You are encouraged to write your answers in the book for future reference.

Supporting graphics Visual cues are given to help you understand the exercises.

Supporting audio This symbol shows that the answers to the exercise are available as audio tracks. Listen to them after completing the exercise.

29.11 SAY THE ANSWERS OUT LOUD, FILLING IN THE GAPS

Has Milo got a washing machine?

No, _he hasn't_.

① Has she got a toaster?

Yes, _____.

② Has the house got a dining room?

Yes, _____.

③ Have they got a new refrigerator?

No, _____.

④ Has it got a large kitchen?

No, _____.

Listening exercise This symbol indicates that you should listen to an audio track in order to answer the questions in the exercise.

45.12 LISTEN TO THE AUDIO AND MARK WHO IS GOOD AT OR BAD AT EACH ACTIVITY

Good at ✓ Bad at ☐

① Good at ☐ Bad at ☐

② Good at ☐ Bad at ☐

③ Good at ☐ Bad at ☐

④ Good at ☐ Bad at ☐

Speaking exercise This symbol indicates that you should say your answers out loud, then compare them to model recordings included in your audio files.

Audio

English for Everyone features extensive supporting audio materials. You are encouraged to use them as much as you can, to improve your understanding of spoken English, and to make your own accent and pronunciation more natural. Each file can be played, paused, and repeated as often as you like, until you are confident you understand what has been said.

LISTENING EXERCISES
This symbol indicates that you should listen to an audio track in order to answer the questions in the exercise.

SUPPORTING AUDIO
This symbol indicates that extra audio material is available for you to listen to after completing the module.

FREE AUDIO
website and app
www.dkefe.com

Track your progress

The course is designed to make it easy to monitor your progress, with regular summary and review modules. Answers are provided for every exercise, so you can see how well you have understood each teaching point.

Checklists Every unit ends with a checklist, where you can check off the new skills you have learned.

08 ✔ CHECKLIST
⚙ "These" and "those" ☐   **Aa** Possessions ☐   Using determiners and pronouns ☐

Review modules At the end of a group of units, you will find a more detailed review module, summarizing the language you have learned.

Check boxes Use these boxes to mark the skills you feel comfortable with. Go back and review anything you feel you need to practice further.

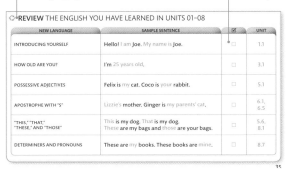

REVIEW THE ENGLISH YOU HAVE LEARNED IN UNITS 01–08

NEW LANGUAGE	SAMPLE SENTENCE	☑	UNIT
INTRODUCING YOURSELF	Hello! I am Joe. My name is Joe.	☐	1.1
HOW OLD ARE YOU?	I'm 25 years old.	☐	3.1
POSSESSIVE ADJECTIVES	Felix is my cat. Coco is your rabbit.	☐	5.1
APOSTROPHE WITH "S"	Lizzie's mother. Ginger is my parents' cat.	☐	6.1, 6.5
"THIS," "THAT," "THESE," AND "THOSE"	This is my dog. That is my dog. These are my bags and those are your bags.	☐	5.6, 8.1
DETERMINERS AND PRONOUNS	These are my books. These books are mine.	☐	8.7

35

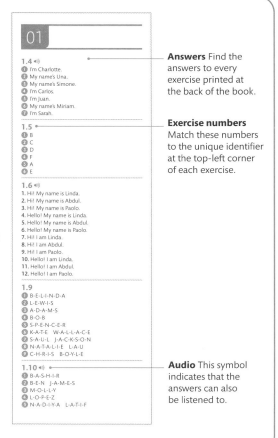

Answers Find the answers to every exercise printed at the back of the book.

Exercise numbers Match these numbers to the unique identifier at the top-left corner of each exercise.

Audio This symbol indicates that the answers can also be listened to.

01

1.4 ◄))
1 I'm Charlotte.
2 My name's Una.
3 My name's Simone.
4 I'm Carlos.
5 I'm Juan.
6 My name's Miriam.
7 I'm Sarah.

1.5
1 B
2 C
3 D
4 F
5 A
6 E

1.6 ◄))
1. Hi! My name is Linda.
2. Hi! My name is Abdul.
3. Hi! My name is Paolo.
4. Hello! My name is Linda.
5. Hello! My name is Abdul.
6. Hello! My name is Paolo.
7. Hi! I am Linda.
8. Hi! I am Abdul.
9. Hi! I am Paolo.
10. Hello! I am Linda.
11. Hello! I am Abdul.
12. Hello! I am Paolo.

1.9
1 B-E-L-I-N-D-A
2 L-E-W-I-S
3 A-D-A-M-S
4 B-O-B
5 S-P-E-N-C-E-R
6 K-A-T-E W-A-L-L-A-C-E
7 S-A-U-L J-A-C-K-S-O-N
8 N-A-T-A-L-I-E L-A-U
9 C-H-R-I-S B-O-Y-L-E

1.10 ◄))
1 B-A-S-H-I-R
2 B-E-N J-A-M-E-S
3 M-O-L-L-Y
4 L-O-P-E-Z
5 N-A-D-I-Y-A L-A-T-I-F

01 Introducing yourself

You can greet people by saying "Hello!" or "Hi!" Introduce yourself using "I am." You may also need to spell out the letters of your name.

⚙ **New language** Using "to be" with names
Aa Vocabulary Names and letters
🧩 **New skill** Saying your name

1.1 KEY LANGUAGE SAYING YOUR NAME

There are different ways of greeting someone and introducing yourself.

This can be a formal or informal greeting.

Hello! I am Lyla.

You can use "I am" plus your name to introduce yourself.

This is an informal greeting. It is often used in casual conversation.

Hi! My name is Joe.

You can also use "my name is" plus your name to introduce yourself.

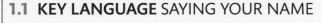

1.2 OTHER WAYS TO SAY YOUR NAME

In conversational English, speakers often use contractions. These are shortened versions of pairs of words.

I am Lyla.

I'm Lyla.

You can contract "I am'" to "I'm."

My name is Joe.

My name's Joe.

You can contract "name is" to "name's."

1.3 HOW TO FORM SAYING YOUR NAME

SUBJECT	"TO BE"	NAME
My name	is	Lyla.
I	am	

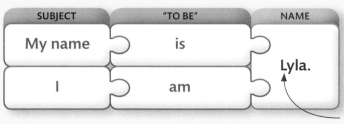

Use a capital letter at the start of a name.

1.4 REWRITE EACH SENTENCE IN ITS CONTRACTED FORM

My name is Jack.
My name's Jack

1 I am Charlotte.

_____

2 My name is Una.

_____

3 My name is Simone.

_____

4 I am Carlos.

_____

5 I am Juan.

_____

6 My name is Miriam.

_____

7 I am Sarah.

_____

1.5 LISTEN TO THE AUDIO, THEN NUMBER THE PEOPLE IN THE ORDER IN WHICH THEY SPEAK

A ☐ Charlie

B ☐1 Katherine

C ☐ JOSEPH

D ☐ Ruby

E ☐ Elliot

F ☐ Oliver

1.6 USE THE CHART TO CREATE 12 CORRECT SENTENCES AND SAY THEM OUT LOUD

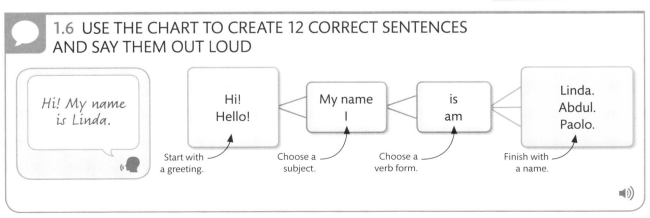

Hi! My name is Linda.

| Hi! Hello! | My name I | is am | Linda. Abdul. Paolo. |

Start with a greeting.   Choose a subject.   Choose a verb form.   Finish with a name.

13

1.7 KEY LANGUAGE SPELLING YOUR NAME

How do you spell your first name?

This is how you ask someone to spell their first name.

My name's Jacob, J-A-C-O-B.

You say each letter.

How do you spell your last name?

This is how you ask someone to spell their last name.

Williams, W-I-L-L-I-A-M-S.

How do you spell your full name?

This is your first name and your last name.

J-A-C-O-B W-I-L-L-I-A-M-S.

1.8 PRONUNCIATION THE ALPHABET

Listen to how the letters of the alphabet are pronounced in English.

Aa Bb Cc Dd Ee Ff Gg Hh Ii
Jj Kk Ll Mm Nn Oo Pp Qq
Rr Ss Tt Uu Vv Ww Xx Yy Zz

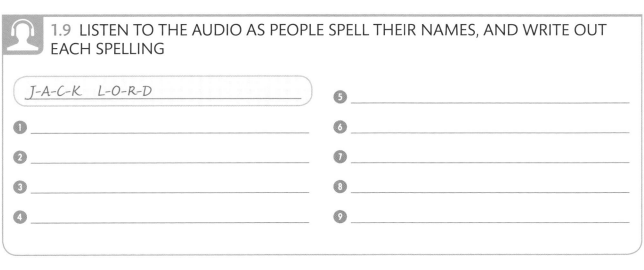

1.9 LISTEN TO THE AUDIO AS PEOPLE SPELL THEIR NAMES, AND WRITE OUT EACH SPELLING

J-A-C-K   L-O-R-D

1 _____

2 _____

3 _____

4 _____

5 _____

6 _____

7 _____

8 _____

9 _____

1.10 SPELL OUT EACH PERSON'S NAME, THEN SAY THE SENTENCES OUT LOUD

My name is Gabriel,
G-A-B-R-I-E-L.

3 My name's Molly,
_____

1 My last name is Bashir,
_____

4 My last name's Lopez,
_____

2 I am Ben James,
_____

5 I'm Nadiya Latif,
_____

01 ✓ CHECKLIST

⚙ Using "to be" with names ☐   **Aa** Names and letters ☐   🧩 Saying your name ☐

15

2.1 COUNTRIES

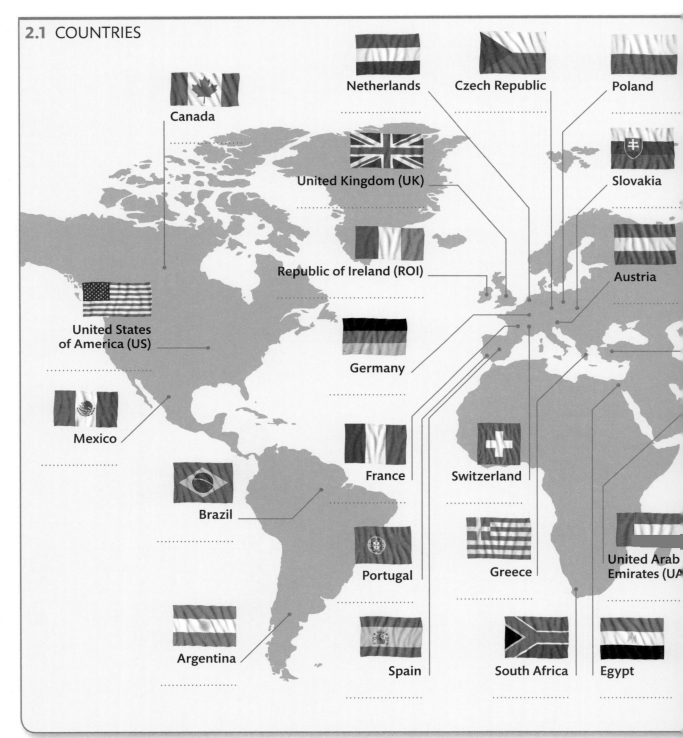

Canada

Netherlands

Czech Republic

Poland

United Kingdom (UK)

Slovakia

Republic of Ireland (ROI)

Austria

United States
of America (US)

Germany

Mexico

France

Switzerland

Brazil

Portugal

Greece

United Arab
Emirates (UA...

Argentina

Spain

South Africa

Egypt

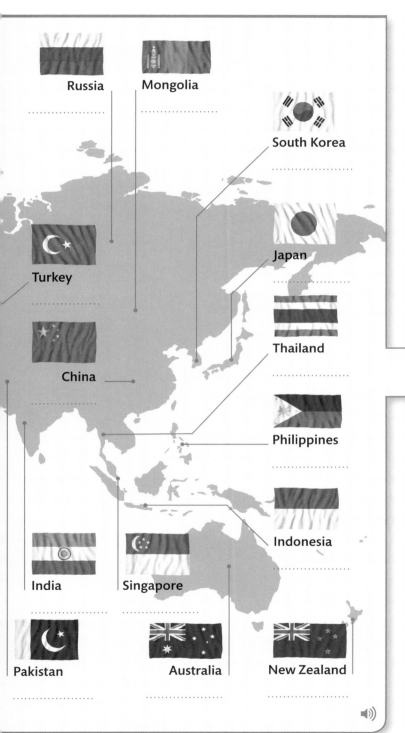

Russia ....

Mongolia ....

South Korea ....

Japan ....

Turkey ....

Thailand ....

China ....

Philippines ....

India ....

Indonesia ....

Singapore ....

Pakistan ....

Australia ....

New Zealand ....

🔊

2.2 NATIONALITIES

USA	➡	American
Canada	➡	Canadian
Mexico	➡	Mexican
Brazil	➡	Brazilian
Argentina	➡	Argentinian
UK	➡	British
France	➡	French
Russia	➡	Russian
Spain	➡	Spanish
Portugal	➡	Portuguese
Poland	➡	Polish
Greece	➡	Greek
Turkey	➡	Turkish
Egypt	➡	Egyptian
China	➡	Chinese
Japan	➡	Japanese
India	➡	Indian
Pakistan	➡	Pakistani
Mongolia	➡	Mongolian
Australia	➡	Australian
Germany	➡	German
Switzerland	➡	Swiss
Austria	➡	Austrian

🔊

03 Talking about yourself

It's useful to know how to say your age and where you come from. You can use the verb "to be" to talk about these topics.

⚙ **New language** "To be" with ages and nationalities
Aa Vocabulary Numbers and nationalities
🧩 **New skill** Talking about yourself

3.1 KEY LANGUAGE SAYING YOUR AGE

Use the verb "to be" to talk about your age.

How old are you?

I am 25 years old.

The verb "to be" changes with the subject.

🔊

3.2 FURTHER EXAMPLES SAYING YOUR AGE

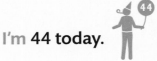

Ruby is seven years old.

I'm 44 today.

Izzy and Chloe are 13.

My grandma is 92 years old.

🔊

3.3 HOW TO FORM SAYING YOUR AGE

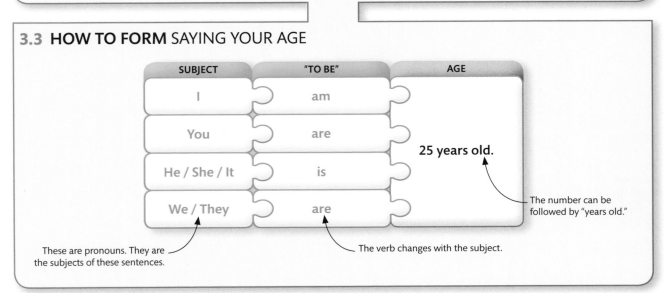

SUBJECT	"TO BE"	AGE
I	am	
You	are	
He / She / It	is	25 years old.
We / They	are	

The number can be followed by "years old."

These are pronouns. They are the subjects of these sentences.

The verb changes with the subject.

3.4 VOCABULARY NUMBERS

1 one	2 two	3 three	4 four	5 five	6 six
7 seven	8 eight	9 nine	10 ten	11 eleven	12 twelve
13 thirteen	14 fourteen	15 fifteen	16 sixteen	17 seventeen	18 eighteen
19 nineteen	20 twenty	21 twenty-one	22 twenty-two	30 thirty	40 forty
50 fifty	60 sixty	70 seventy	80 eighty	90 ninety	100 one hundred

🔊

Aa 3.5 WRITE THE NUMBERS AS WORDS

3 = _three_

1. 11 = _____

2. 17 = _____

3. 34 = _____

4. 59 = _____

5. 85 = _____

🔊

3.6 FILL IN THE GAPS WITH THE CORRECT FORMS OF "TO BE"

Michael _____ is _____ 32 years old.

1. Theo _____ 45 years old.

2. Madison _____ 27 years old.

3. Jeremy and Tanya _____ 90 years old.

4. We _____ 29 years old.

5. I _____ 34 years old.

🔊

19

3.7 PRONUNCIATION SIMILAR SOUNDING NUMBERS

It is important to stress the correct syllable in these numbers.

Stress the last syllables.

Stress the first syllables.

13 Thir**teen**	30 **Thir**ty
14 Four**teen**	40 **For**ty
15 Fif**teen**	50 **Fif**ty
16 Six**teen**	60 **Six**ty
17 Seven**teen**	70 **Seven**ty
18 Eigh**teen**	80 **Eigh**ty
19 Nine**teen**	90 **Nine**ty

3.8 LISTEN TO THE AUDIO AND MARK THE CORRECT AGES

Tamar	**15** ☐	**50** ☑
❶ Bobby	**14** ☐	**40** ☐
❷ Carl	**13** ☐	**30** ☐
❸ Lia	**19** ☐	**90** ☐
❹ Sam	**16** ☐	**60** ☐
❺ Molly	**18** ☐	**80** ☐
❻ Justin	**17** ☐	**70** ☐
❼ Ada	**13** ☐	**30** ☐

3.9 KEY LANGUAGE SAYING WHERE YOU'RE FROM

There are different ways of saying where you are from.

"Where" is the question word for place.

Remember, "to be" changes with the subject.

This describes the country that you belong to.

You use an adjective to talk about nationality.

Where are you from?

I am from Spain.

What nationality are you?

I'm Spanish.

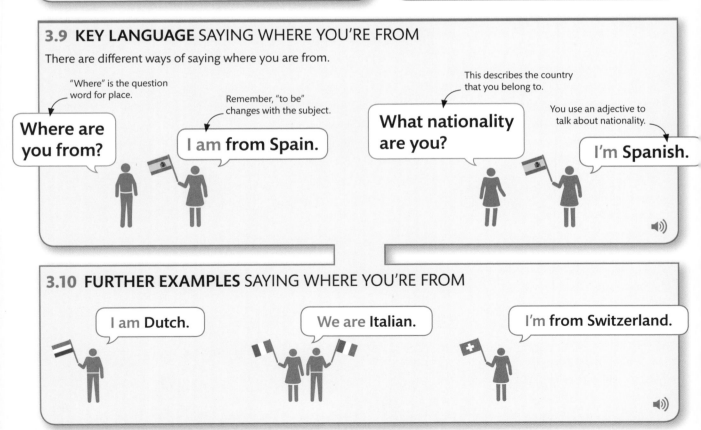

3.10 FURTHER EXAMPLES SAYING WHERE YOU'RE FROM

I am Dutch.

We are Italian.

I'm from Switzerland.

3.11 HOW TO FORM SAYING WHERE YOU'RE FROM

I + "TO BE"	"FROM"	COUNTRY
I am	from	Spain.

You use the noun after ""from."

I + "TO BE"	NATIONALITY
I am	Spanish.

Here you use the adjective.

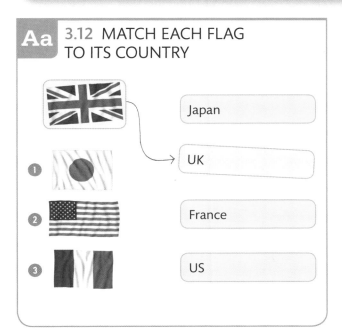

Aa 3.12 MATCH EACH FLAG TO ITS COUNTRY

Japan

UK

France

US

1
2
3

3.13 WRITE THE NATIONALITY FOR EACH COUNTRY

Italy	=	_Italian_
❶ Spain	=	_____
❷ Germany	=	_____
❸ Canada	=	_____
❹ America	=	_____
❺ Australia	=	_____
❻ China	=	_____

🔊

3.14 USE THE CHART TO CREATE 12 CORRECT SENTENCES AND SAY THEM OUT LOUD

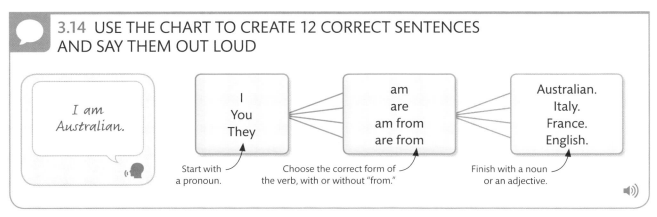

I am Australian.

I	am
You	are
They	am from
	are from

Australian.
Italy.
France.
English.

Start with a pronoun.

Choose the correct form of the verb, with or without "from."

Finish with a noun or an adjective.

🔊

---

03 ✔ CHECKLIST

⚙ "To be" with ages and nationalities ☐   **Aa** Numbers and nationalities ☐   🧩 Talking about yourself ☐

21

Vocabulary

4.1 PABLO'S FAMILY

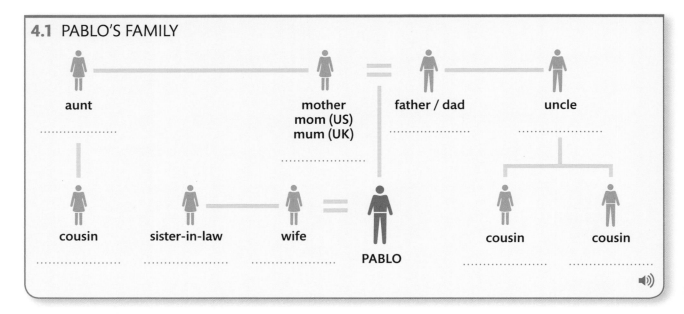

aunt

mother
mom (US)
mum (UK)

father / dad

uncle

cousin

sister-in-law

wife

PABLO

cousin

cousin

4.2 MARY'S FAMILY

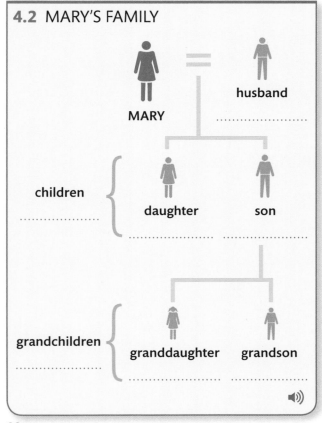

husband

MARY

children

daughter

son

grandchildren

granddaughter

grandson

4.3 SARAH'S FAMILY

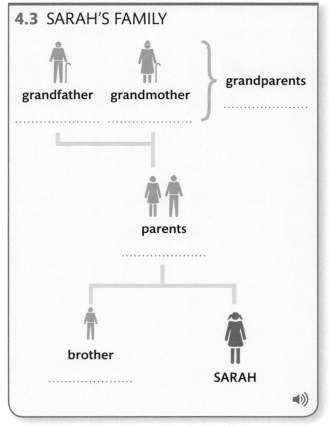

grandfather

grandmother

grandparents

parents

brother

SARAH

4.4 DAN'S FAMILY

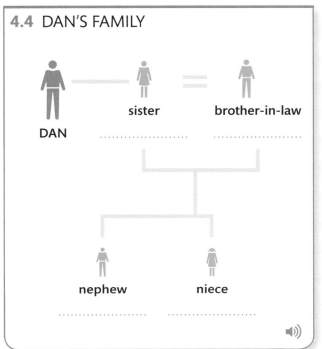

DAN — sister = brother-in-law

nephew   niece

4.5 HARRY'S FAMILY

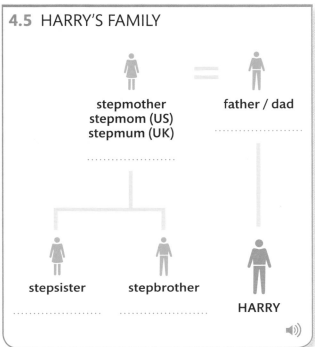

stepmother stepmom (US) stepmum (UK) = father / dad

stepsister   stepbrother   HARRY

4.6 PETS AND DOMESTIC ANIMALS

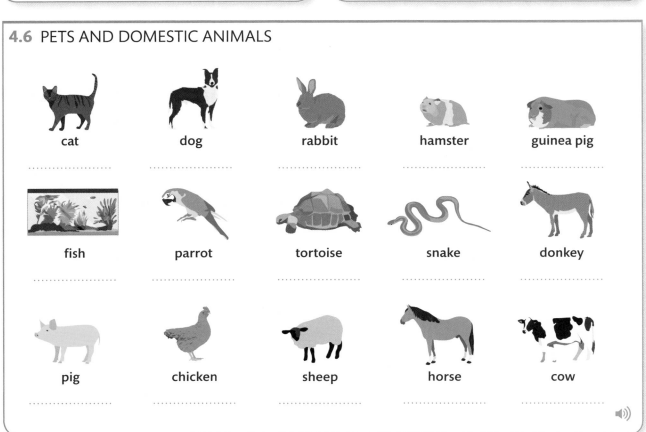

cat   dog   rabbit   hamster   guinea pig

fish   parrot   tortoise   snake   donkey

pig   chicken   sheep   horse   cow

05 Things you have

Possessive adjectives tell you who something (such as a pet) belongs to. "This" and "that" are determiners. They point out a specific object or person.

⚙ **New language** Possessive adjectives; "this" and "that"
Aa Vocabulary Animals and family
🧩 **New skill** Talking about who things belong to

5.1 KEY LANGUAGE POSSESSIVE ADJECTIVES

Possessive adjectives are used before the noun. They change depending on whether the owner is singular, plural, male or female, the person you are talking to, or yourself.

Felix is my cat.

↳ I own the cat.

Buster is her dog.
↳ The dog belongs to a woman.

Rachel is our daughter.

↳ We are her parents.

Coco is your rabbit.

↳ The rabbit belongs to you.

Polly is his parrot.

↳ The parrot belongs to a man.

John is their son.

↳ They are his parents.

🔊

5.2 HOW TO FORM POSSESSIVE ADJECTIVES

I	you	he	she	it	we	they
⬇	⬇	⬇	⬇	⬇	⬇	⬇
my	your	his	her	its	our	their
⬇	⬇	⬇	⬇	⬇	⬇	⬇
my cat	your rabbit	his wife	her sister	its ball	our horse	their son

🔊

5.3 MATCH THE PICTURES TO THE PHRASES

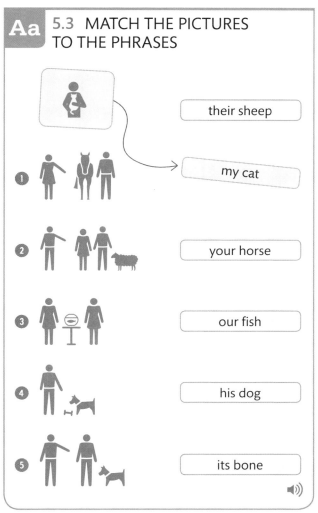

their sheep

my cat

your horse

our fish

his dog

its bone

5.4 FILL IN THE GAPS USING THE CORRECT POSSESSIVE ADJECTIVES

_____ _Her_ _____ (She) name is Mary.

1. Bingo is _____ (I) dog.

2. _____ (She) aunt is called Goldie.

3. _____ (I) cat eats fish.

4. _____ (They) rabbit lives in the backyard.

5. _____ (We) parrot is from Colombia.

6. _____ (He) wife is called Henrietta.

7. _____ (They) dog is 10 years old.

8. _____ (We) aunt lives on a farm in Ohio.

9. Here is _____ (it) ball.

5.5 REWRITE THE SENTENCES, CORRECTING THE ERRORS

Nick **are** my brother.
Nick is my brother.

1. Farida **are** their sister.
_____

2. Duke **am** our dog.
_____

3. Daisy **are** her mother.
_____

4. They **is** his grandparents.
_____

5. It **am** our horse.
_____

6. John **am** our cousin.
_____

7. I **are** Daisy's daughter.
_____

8. You **is** my friend.
_____

5.6 KEY LANGUAGE "THIS" AND "THAT"

"This" and "that" are called determiners. They point out a specific object you want to talk about. Use "this" for something close to you. Use "that" for something farther away.

 This is my dog.

The dog is close to you.

That is my dog.

The dog is farther away from you.

5.7 FURTHER EXAMPLES "THIS" AND "THAT"

This is your rabbit.

This is her horse.

This is its bed.

That is your rabbit.

That is her horse.

That is its bed.

5.8 FILL IN THE GAPS WITH "THIS" OR "THAT"

 _____That_____ is my dog.

③   _____ is their pig.

① _____ is her horse.

④  _____ is his cow.

② _____ is our rabbit.

⑤ _____ is your fish.

26

5.9 REWRITE THE SENTENCES, PUTTING THE WORDS IN THE CORRECT ORDER

is	horse.	This	his

This is his horse.

① | their | Lily | is | sister. |

_____

② | son | old. | 12 | is | years | Our |

_____

③ | cow. | their | is | That |

_____

④ | is | ball. | your | This |

_____

⑤ | called | Her | Caspar. | father | is |

_____

5.10 LISTEN TO THE AUDIO, THEN NUMBER THE IMAGES IN THE ORDER THEY ARE DESCRIBED

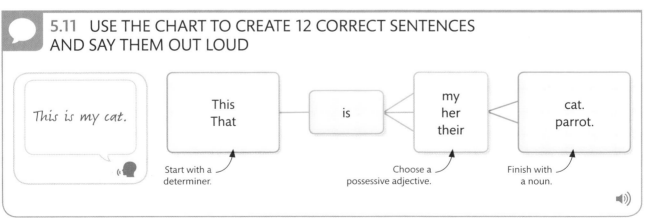

5.11 USE THE CHART TO CREATE 12 CORRECT SENTENCES AND SAY THEM OUT LOUD

This is my cat.

| This / That | is | my / her / their | cat. / parrot. |

Start with a determiner.

Choose a possessive adjective.

Finish with a noun.

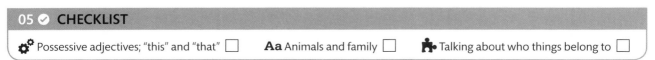

05 ✓ CHECKLIST

⚙ Possessive adjectives; "this" and "that" ☐   **Aa** Animals and family ☐   🧩 Talking about who things belong to ☐

27

06 Using apostrophes

In English, you can use apostrophes (') to show belonging. You can use them to show who owns something, such as a pet, and to talk about your family.

⚙ **New language** Possessive apostrophe
Aa Vocabulary Family and pets
🧩 **New skill** Talking about belonging

6.1 KEY LANGUAGE APOSTROPHE WITH "S"

Add an apostrophe and the letter "s" to the end of a singular noun to show that what comes after the noun belongs to it.

This form is correct in English, but it is not normally used.

the mother of Lizzie

Lizzie's mother

This is a common way of talking about belonging.

An apostrophe with an "s" shows ownership.

6.2 FURTHER EXAMPLES APOSTROPHE WITH "S"

Dave's **grandmother**

The dog's **ball**

Tess's **dog**

This can also be written Tess'.

Juan and Beth's **parrot**

If something belongs to more than one noun, only add "-'s" to the last one.

6.3 REWRITE THE PHRASES USING AN APOSTROPHE PLUS "S"

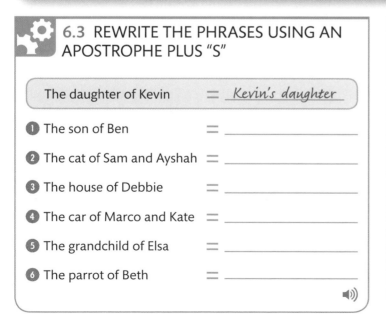

| The daughter of Kevin | = | _Kevin's daughter_ |

❶ The son of Ben = _____

❷ The cat of Sam and Ayshah = _____

❸ The house of Debbie = _____

❹ The car of Marco and Kate = _____

❺ The grandchild of Elsa = _____

❻ The parrot of Beth = _____

6.4 LISTEN TO THE AUDIO AND MATCH THE PAIRS

Edith is — Ben's mother.

❶ Lucas is → Ben's grandmother.

❷ Lily is — Ben's son.

❸ Noah is — Ben's sister.

❹ Grace is — Ben's brother

❺ Alex is — Ben's father.

6.5 KEY LANGUAGE APOSTROPHES AND PLURAL NOUNS

To show belonging with a plural noun, just add an apostrophe with no "s."

Ginger is my parents' cat.

Plural nouns use an apostrophe with no "s."

6.6 FURTHER EXAMPLES APOSTROPHES AND PLURAL NOUNS

This is my cousins' **rabbit.**

That is his grandparents' **house.**

Rex is her brothers' **dog.**

Polly is our children's **parrot.**

For plural nouns that don't end "s," you should still add "-'s."

6.7 REWRITE PUTTING THE WORDS IN THE CORRECT ORDER

| uncle. | Kevin | Sharon's | is |

Kevin is Sharon's uncle.

1. | Skanda's | is | wife. | Angela |

_____

2. | snake. | is | my cousins' | That |

_____

3. | Sue | aunt. | Ella and Mark's | is |

_____

4. | is | John's | cat. | Ginger |

_____

6.8 SAY THE SENTENCES OUT LOUD, FILLING IN THE GAPS

Edith is _____Ben's_____ (Ben) grandmother.

1. Kathy is _____ (Dave) aunt.

2. Rex is _____ (Noah and Pat) dog.

3. This is _____ (her cousins) house.

4. Felix is _____ (the children) cat.

---

06 ✓ **CHECKLIST**

⚙ Possessive apostrophe ☐   **Aa** Family and pets ☐   🧩 Talking about belonging ☐

07 Vocabulary

7.1 EVERYDAY THINGS

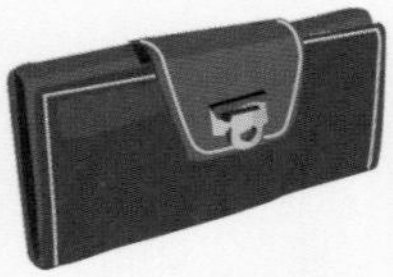

**wallet (US)
purse (UK)**

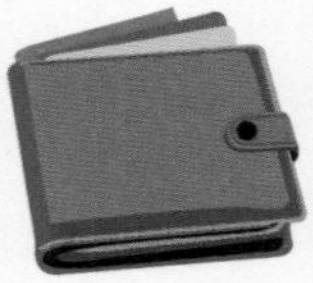

wallet

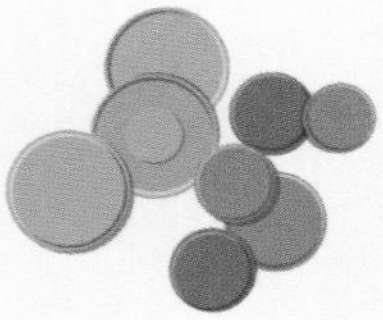

coins

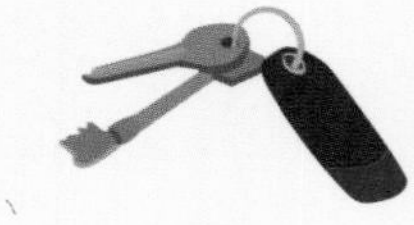

keys

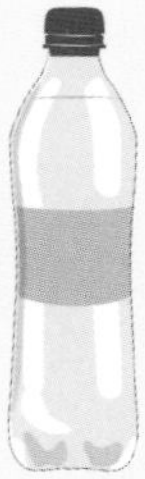

bottle of water

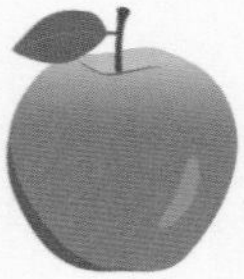

apple

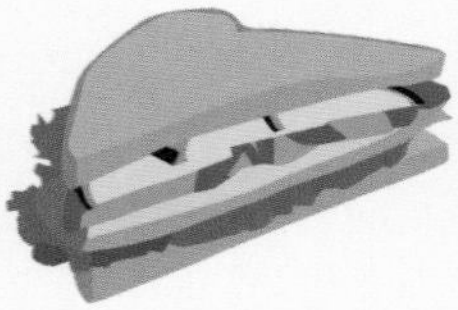

sandwich

**cell phone (US)
mobile phone (UK)**

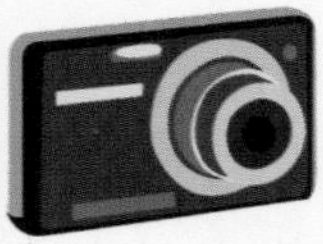

camera

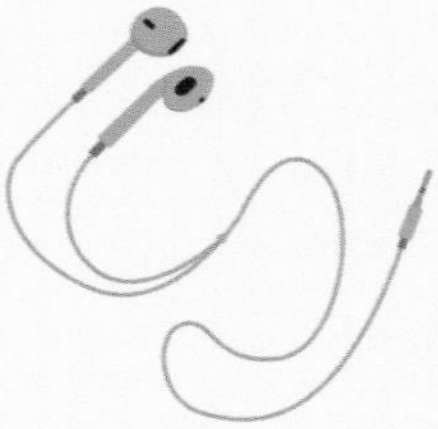

earphones

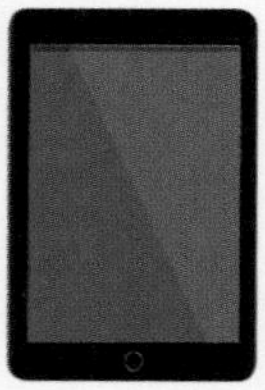

tablet

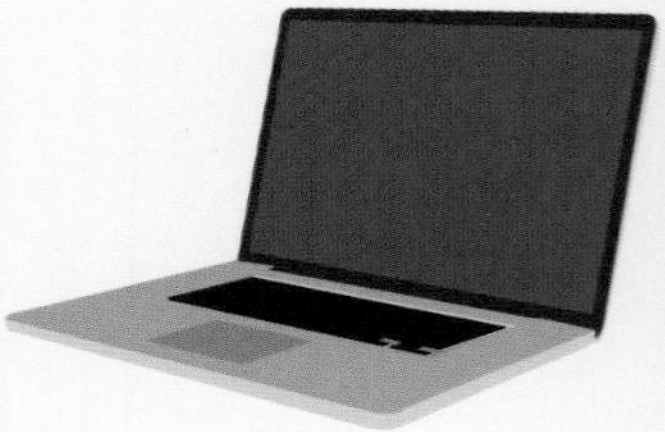

laptop

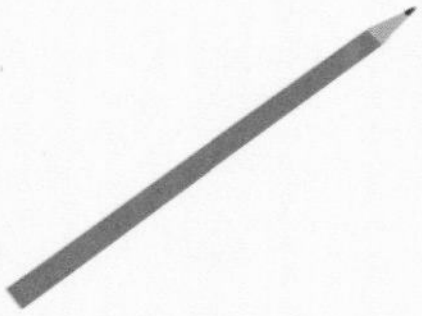

pencil

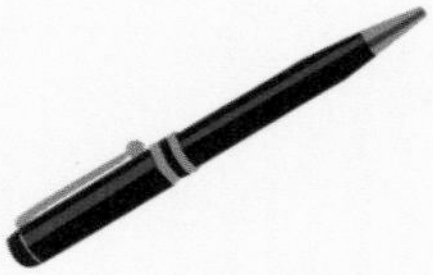

pen

notebook

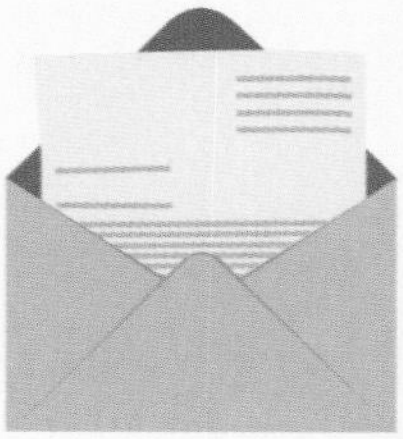

letter

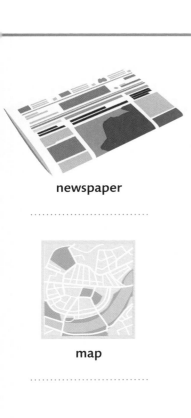
newspaper

magazine

book / novel

dictionary

map

mirror

toothbrush

umbrella

hairbrush

planner (US)
diary (UK)

glasses

sunglasses

necklace

watch

passport

ID card

08 Talking about your things

You use "these" and "those" when you are referring to more than one thing. To show who owns a thing, you can use determiners or possessive pronouns.

⚙ **New language** "These" and "those"
Aa Vocabulary Possessions
🧩 **New skill** Using determiners and pronouns

8.1 KEY LANGUAGE USING "THESE" AND "THOSE"

Use "this" for something near you.
This is my bag.

Use "that" for something far from you.
That is my bag.

"These" is the plural of "this."
These are my bags.

"Those" is the plural of "that."
Those are my bags.

Use "these" and "those" for contrast, too. "These" things belong to one person.

"Those" things belong to another person.

These are my bags and those are your bags.

🔊

8.2 CROSS OUT THE INCORRECT WORD IN EACH SENTENCE

This / ~~These~~ is my bag.

1 **This / These** are Diego's keys.

2 **This / These** is Olivia's purse.

3 **That / Those** are my books.

4 **This / These** are my pencils.

5 **That / Those** is Anna's sandwich.

6 **Those / That** is Malik's phone.

🔊

8.3 WRITE EACH SENTENCE IN ITS OTHER FORM

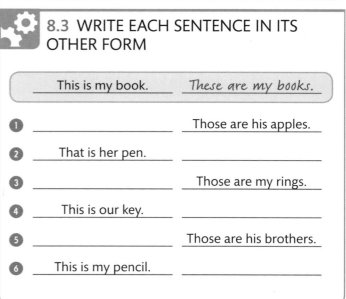

| This is my book. | *These are my books.* |

1 _____ | Those are his apples.

2 That is her pen. | _____

3 _____ | Those are my rings.

4 This is our key. | _____

5 _____ | Those are his brothers.

6 This is my pencil. | _____

8.4 **VOCABULARY** SPELLING RULES FOR PLURALS

For most nouns, to make the plural you add "s."

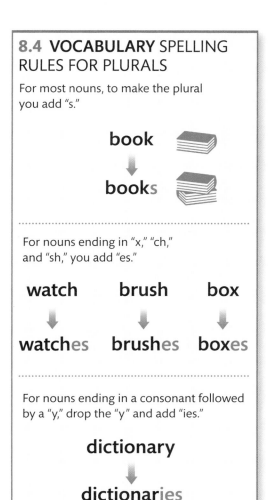

book

↓

books

For nouns ending in "x," "ch," and "sh," you add "es."

watch   brush   box

↓   ↓   ↓

watches brushes boxes

For nouns ending in a consonant followed by a "y," drop the "y" and add "ies."

dictionary

↓

dictionaries

🔊

Aa 8.5 FIND EIGHT PLURALS IN THE GRID AND WRITE THEM IN GROUPS

```
W A T C H E S O B W O A D
A B P X E I N G A Q E P I
N D E M B R U S H E S P A
N E C K L A C E S A C L R
S A N D W I C H E S I E I
D I C T I O N A R I E S E
B O T T L E S Z I S R E S
P Q I W T I O S Y U R D S
T L E L L S H B N E Y S I
```

"S" PLURALS: **"ES" PLURALS:**   **"IES" PLURALS:**

① _necklaces_   ④ _____   ⑦ _____

② _____   ⑤ _____   ⑧ _____

③ _____   ⑥ _____

🔊

Aa 8.6 WRITE A PLURAL TO DESCRIBE EACH PICTURE

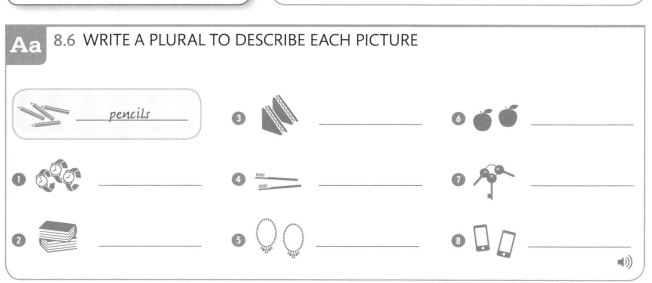

pencils

① _____   ③ _____   ⑥ _____

② _____   ④ _____   ⑦ _____

⑤ _____   ⑧ _____

🔊

8.7 KEY LANGUAGE DETERMINERS AND PRONOUNS

You can use determiners or possessive pronouns to explain who owns something.

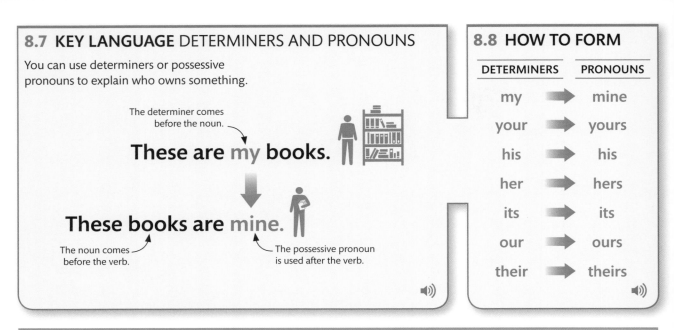

The determiner comes before the noun.

These are my books.

These books are mine.

The noun comes before the verb.

The possessive pronoun is used after the verb.

8.8 HOW TO FORM

DETERMINERS		PRONOUNS
my	➡	mine
your	➡	yours
his	➡	his
her	➡	hers
its	➡	its
our	➡	ours
their	➡	theirs

8.9 FILL IN THE GAPS TO WRITE EACH SENTENCE TWO OTHER WAYS

These are Aman's books.	These are his books.	These books are his.
1 This is Leesa's laptop.		
2 Those are Una and Ben's keys.		
3 These are Jo's and my passports.		
4 That is John's brush.		

8.10 LISTEN TO THE AUDIO, THEN WRITE EACH NOUN IN THE CORRECT GROUP

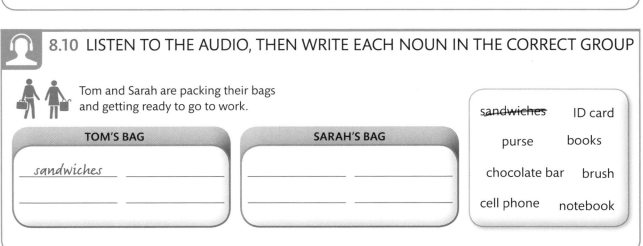

Tom and Sarah are packing their bags and getting ready to go to work.

TOM'S BAG

sandwiches

SARAH'S BAG

~~sandwiches~~   ID card

purse   books

chocolate bar   brush

cell phone   notebook

8.11 USE THE CHART TO CREATE 12 CORRECT SENTENCES AND SAY THEM OUT LOUD

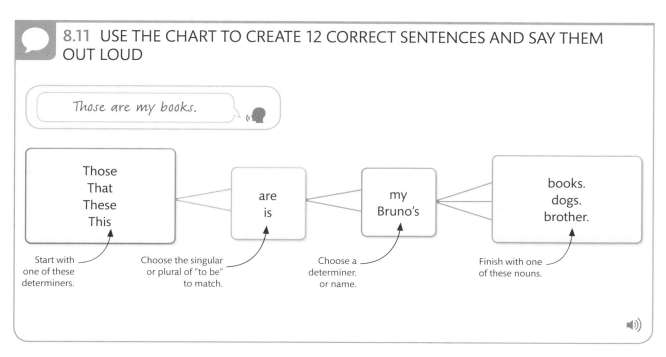

Those are my books.

| Those / That / These / This | are / is | my / Bruno's | books. / dogs. / brother. |

Start with one of these determiners.

Choose the singular or plural of "to be" to match.

Choose a determiner. or name.

Finish with one of these nouns.

08 ✓ CHECKLIST

⚙ "These" and "those" ☐   **Aa** Possessions ☐   🧩 Using determiners and pronouns ☐

♻ REVIEW THE ENGLISH YOU HAVE LEARNED IN UNITS 01–08

NEW LANGUAGE	SAMPLE SENTENCE	☑	UNIT
INTRODUCING YOURSELF	**Hello!** I am **Joe.** My name is **Joe.**	☐	1.1
HOW OLD ARE YOU?	**I'm** 25 years old.	☐	3.1
POSSESSIVE ADJECTIVES	**Felix is** my **cat. Coco is** your **rabbit.**	☐	5.1
APOSTROPHE WITH "S"	Lizzie's **mother. Ginger is** my parents' **cat.**	☐	6.1, 6.5
"THIS," "THAT," "THESE," AND "THOSE"	This **is my dog.** That **is my dog.** These **are my bags and** those **are your bags.**	☐	5.6, 8.1
DETERMINERS AND PRONOUNS	**These are** my **books. These books are** mine.	☐	8.7

35

9.1 JOBS

cleaner

driver

sales assistant

hairdresser

chef

gardener

vet

actor

doctor

nurse

dentist

police officer

fire fighter

farmer

construction worker (US)
builder (UK)

artist

receptionist

mechanic

engineer

scientist

teacher

businesswoman

businessman

waiter

waitress

electrician

pilot

judge

9.2 PLURALS

Most nouns about people and jobs are made plural in the usual way by adding "-s" or "-es".

driver → **drivers**

waitress → **waitresses**

Nouns that end in "man" change to end in "men" in the plural.

man → **men**

woman → **women**

businessman → **businessmen**

businesswoman → **businesswomen**

For nouns made up of two words, the second word is made plural.

police officer → **police officers**

10 Talking about your job

You can use the verb "to be" to describe your job. The verb "to work" can give more information about where you work and who you work with.

⚙ **New language** Using "I am" for your job
Aa Vocabulary Jobs and workplaces
🧩 **New skill** Describing your job

10.1 KEY LANGUAGE YOUR JOB

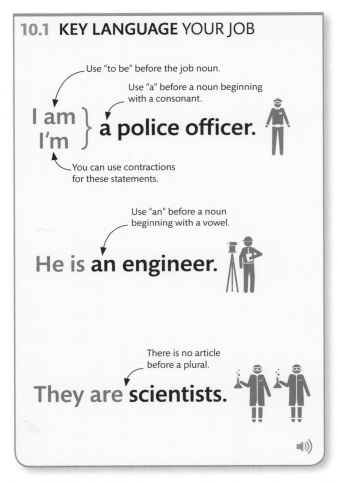

Use "to be" before the job noun.

Use "a" before a noun beginning with a consonant.

I am
I'm } **a police officer.**

You can use contractions for these statements.

Use "an" before a noun beginning with a vowel.

He is an engineer.

There is no article before a plural.

They are scientists.

10.2 FILL IN THE GAPS WITH THE CORRECT VERB AND ARTICLE

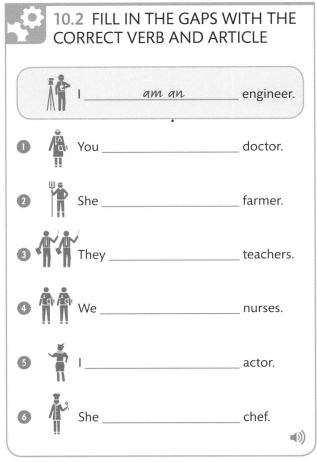

I _____ *am an* _____ engineer.

1. You _____ doctor.

2. She _____ farmer.

3. They _____ teachers.

4. We _____ nurses.

5. I _____ actor.

6. She _____ chef.

10.3 CROSS OUT THE INCORRECT WORD IN EACH SENTENCE

They ~~are~~ / is farmers.

1. You are / is a driver.

2. I am / is a mechanic.

3. He is / are a vet.

4. We am / are sales assistants.

5. They is / are businesswomen.

6. She is / are a waitress.

7. We is / are receptionists.

8. She is / are a gardener.

10.4 **VOCABULARY** WORKPLACES

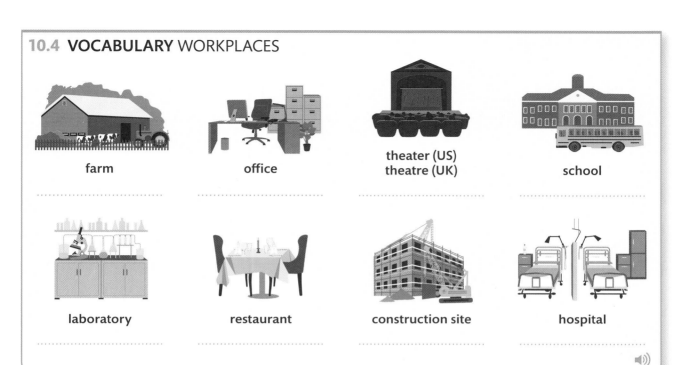

farm

office

theater (US)
theatre (UK)

school

laboratory

restaurant

construction site

hospital

Aa 10.5 MATCH THE JOBS TO THE WORKPLACES

businessman	farm
① nurse	restaurant
② farmer	office
③ scientist	hospital
④ waiter	laboratory
⑤ teacher	construction site
⑥ builder	school
⑦ doctor	theater
⑧ actor	restaurant
⑨ chef	hospital

10.6 **KEY LANGUAGE** INSIDE / OUTSIDE

Use "inside" for jobs in buildings.

A scientist works inside.

Use "outside" for jobs in the open air.

A farmer works outside.

Aa 10.7 MARK THE CORRECT ANSWERS

A hairdresser works outside.	True ☐	False ☑
① A driver works outside.	True ☐	False ☐
② A chef works outside.	True ☐	False ☐
③ A doctor works inside.	True ☐	False ☐
④ A gardener works outside.	True ☐	False ☐

39

10.8 KEY LANGUAGE USING "WORK IN" AND "WORK ON"

Use "work in" for the locations of most jobs.

I work in a hospital.

I work on a farm. I work on construction sites.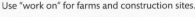

Use "work on" for farms and construction sites.

10.9 LISTEN TO THE AUDIO AND NUMBER THE IMAGES IN THE ORDER THEY ARE DESCRIBED

A ☐

C 1

E ☐

B ☐

D ☐

F ☐

10.10 WRITE TWO SENTENCES TO DESCRIBE EACH PICTURE

Tom _is a farmer._
He works on a farm.

② We _____
_____

④ He _____
_____

① She _____
_____

③ You _____
_____

⑤ Chloe _____
_____

40

10.11 KEY LANGUAGE "WORK WITH"

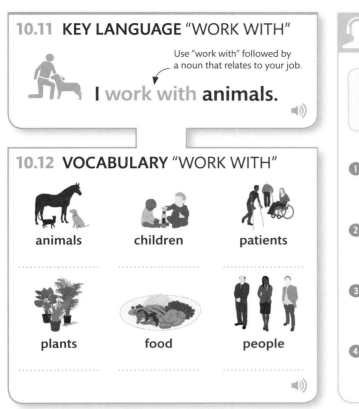

Use "work with" followed by a noun that relates to your job.

I work with **animals.** 🔊

10.12 VOCABULARY "WORK WITH"

animals

children

patients

plants

food

people

🔊

10.13 LISTEN TO THE AUDIO AND MATCH THE PEOPLE TO THEIR JOBS

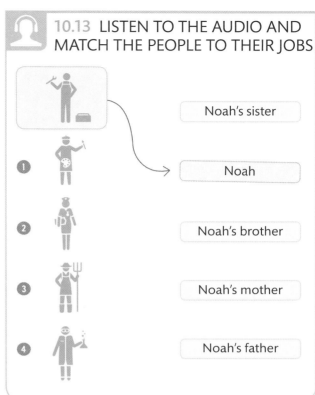

Noah's sister

Noah

1

2

Noah's brother

3

Noah's mother

4

Noah's father

10.14 SAY THE SENTENCES OUT LOUD, FILLING IN THE GAPS

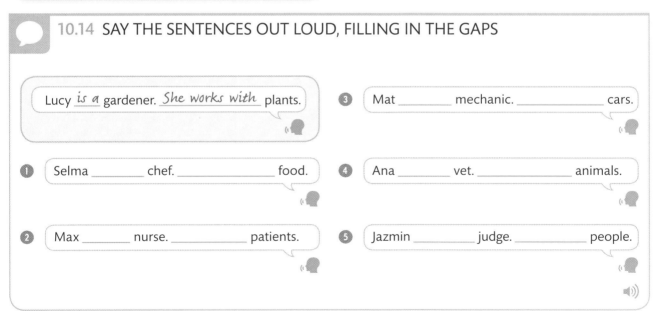

Lucy *is a* gardener. *She works with* plants.

1 Selma _____ chef. _____ food.

2 Max _____ nurse. _____ patients.

3 Mat _____ mechanic. _____ cars.

4 Ana _____ vet. _____ animals.

5 Jazmin _____ judge. _____ people.

🔊

10 ✓ CHECKLIST

⚙ Using "I am" for your job ☐   **Aa** Jobs and workplaces ☐   🧩 Describing your job ☐

11 Telling the time

There are two ways of saying the time in English. You can use hours and minutes, or you can say the minutes first and state their relation to the hour.

⚙ **New language** Times of day
Aa Vocabulary Words for time
🧩 **New skill** Saying what the time is

11.1 KEY LANGUAGE TELLING THE TIME

Use the verb "to be" when giving or asking the time in English.

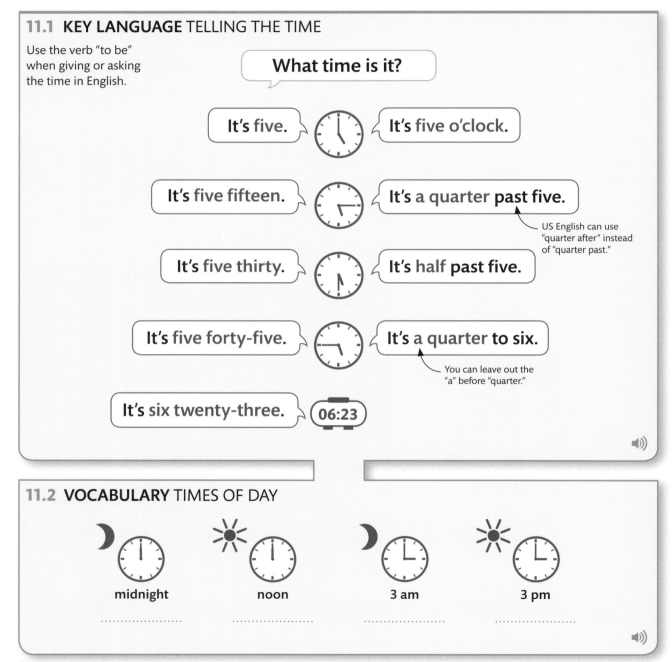

What time is it?

It's five.   It's five o'clock.

It's five fifteen.   It's a quarter **past** five.

US English can use "quarter after" instead of "quarter past."

It's five thirty.   It's **half past** five.

It's five forty-five.   It's a quarter **to** six.

You can leave out the "a" before "quarter."

It's six twenty-three.   06:23

11.2 VOCABULARY TIMES OF DAY

midnight   noon   3 am   3 pm

Aa 11.3 MATCH THE CLOCKS TO THE TIME PHRASES

- It's midnight.
- ① **12:00** It's seven o'clock.
- ② It's two thirty.
- ③ **11:45** It's half past three.
- ④ It's ten thirty.
- ⑤ **09:15** It's quarter to twelve.
- ⑥ It's a quarter past nine.

🔊

11.4 LISTEN TO THE AUDIO AND MARK THE TIMES YOU HEAR

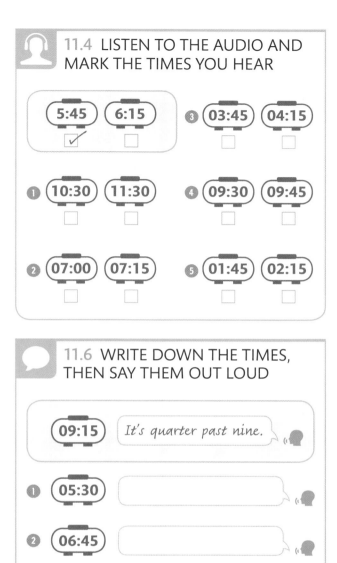

- **5:45** ✓ **6:15** ☐   ③ **03:45** ☐ **04:15** ☐
- ① **10:30** ☐ **11:30** ☐   ④ **09:30** ☐ **09:45** ☐
- ② **07:00** ☐ **07:15** ☐   ⑤ **01:45** ☐ **02:15** ☐

11.6 WRITE DOWN THE TIMES, THEN SAY THEM OUT LOUD

- **09:15** It's quarter past nine. 🔊
- ① **05:30**
- ② **06:45**
- ③ **11:35**
- ④ **08:15**
- ⑤ **10:22**

🔊

⚙ 11.5 WRITE THE TIMES IN FIGURES

It's a quarter to five.	=	4:45

- ① It's nine o'clock. = _____
- ② It's one fifteen. = _____
- ③ It's three twenty-five. = _____
- ④ It's half past two. = _____
- ⑤ It's a quarter past twelve. = _____

🔊

12 Vocabulary

12.1 DAILY ROUTINES

wake up

get up

**take a shower (US)
have a shower (UK)**

**take a bath (US)
have a bath (UK)**

brush your hair

**have breakfast /
eat breakfast**

go to work

go to school

buy groceries

go home

cook dinner

**have dinner /
eat dinner**

12.2 TIMES OF THE DAY

day

night

dawn

morning

 iron a shirt

 get dressed

 brush your teeth

 wash your face

 start work

 have lunch /
eat lunch

 finish work

 leave work

 clear the table

 do the dishes (US)
wash the dishes (UK)

 walk the dog

 go to bed

 afternoon

dusk

evening

late evening

45

13 Describing your day

Use the present simple tense to talk about the things you do regularly: for example, when you normally go to work or eat lunch.

🔧 **New language** The present simple
Aa Vocabulary Routine activities
🧩 **New skill** Talking about your daily routine

13.1 KEY LANGUAGE THE PRESENT SIMPLE

To make the present simple, use the base form of the verb (the infinitive without "to").

The base form of the verb "to eat."

I eat lunch at noon every day.

She eats lunch at 2pm every day.

With he, she, and it, add "s" to the base form.

13.2 FURTHER EXAMPLES THE PRESENT SIMPLE

You **get** up at 7 o'clock.

We **start** work at 9 o'clock.

They **leave** work at 5pm.

She **gets** up at 5:30am.

He **starts** work at 11am.

Rob **leaves** work at 7pm.

13.3 HOW TO FORM THE PRESENT SIMPLE

The base form of the verb.

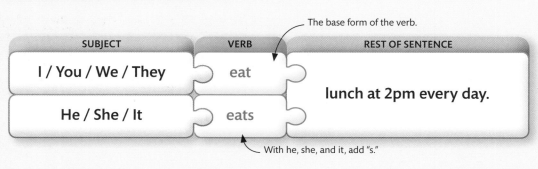

SUBJECT	VERB	REST OF SENTENCE
I / You / We / They	eat	lunch at 2pm every day.
He / She / It	eats	

With he, she, and it, add "s."

13.4 CROSS OUT THE INCORRECT WORD IN EACH SENTENCE

She ~~eat~~ / eats dinner in the evening.

1. He wake up / wakes up at 7 o'clock.
2. You leave / leaves home at 8:30am.
3. I start / starts work at 10am.
4. Ellen get / gets up at 5 o'clock.

5. My wife take / takes a shower in the evening.
6. I take / takes a shower in the morning.
7. My parents eat / eats lunch at 2pm.
8. We leave / leaves work at 4pm.
9. My brother work / works with animals.

13.5 FILL IN THE GAPS USING THE WORDS IN THE PANEL

Michael _____gets_____ up at 7am.

1. I _____ work at 5:30pm.
2. Phil _____ lunch at 12:30pm.
3. We _____ up at 8am.
4. His son _____ work at 5am.
5. My sister _____ work at 7pm.
6. They _____ dinner at 10pm.

~~gets~~   get   starts

leaves   eat   eats   leave

13.6 SAY THE SENTENCES OUT LOUD, FILLING IN THE GAPS

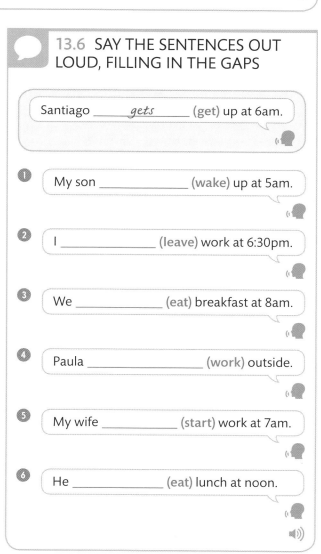

Santiago _____gets_____ (get) up at 6am.

1. My son _____ (wake) up at 5am.
2. I _____ (leave) work at 6:30pm.
3. We _____ (eat) breakfast at 8am.
4. Paula _____ (work) outside.
5. My wife _____ (start) work at 7am.
6. He _____ (eat) lunch at noon.

13.7 KEY LANGUAGE "S" AND "ES" ENDINGS

With some verbs you add "es" for he, she, and it. These
include verbs ending "sh," "ch," "o," "ss," "x," and "z."

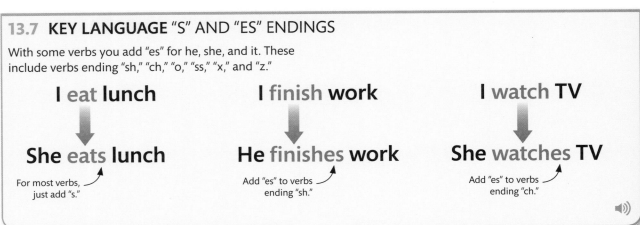

I eat lunch

She eats lunch

For most verbs,
just add "s."

I finish work

He finishes work

Add "es" to verbs
ending "sh."

I watch TV

She watches TV

Add "es" to verbs
ending "ch."

13.8 PRONUNCIATION SAYING "S" AND "ES"

The "-s" endings are pronounced
different ways. Listen to the difference.

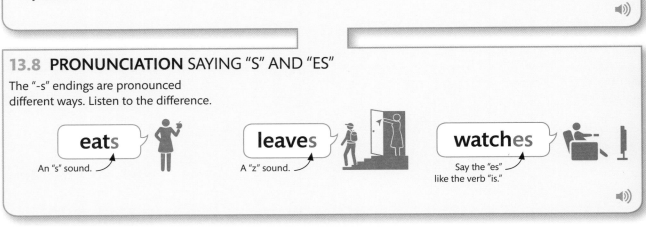

eats

An "s" sound.

leaves

A "z" sound.

watches

Say the "es"
like the verb "is."

13.9 SAY THE WORDS OUT LOUD

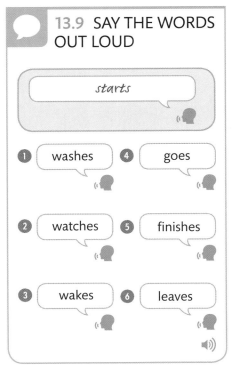

starts

1. washes
4. goes
2. watches
5. finishes
3. wakes
6. leaves

13.10 FILL IN THE GAPS BY PUTTING THE VERBS IN THE CORRECT FORM

He ____*finishes*____ (finish) work at 5 o'clock.

1. Lucia _____ (wake) up at 7am.

2. I _____ (get) up at 7:30am.

3. Ethan _____ (go) to work at 5am.

4. You _____ (leave) work at 5pm.

5. Shona _____ (watch) TV in the evening.

13.11 REWRITE THE SENTENCES, CORRECTING THE ERRORS

Our children **eats** breakfast at 8am.
Our children eat breakfast at 8am.

❶ My mother **watchs** TV in the morning.

_____

❷ We **goes** to bed at midnight.

_____

❸ My husband **finishs** work at 6:30pm.

_____

❹ Rob **go** to work at 8:30am.

_____

❺ I **takes** a shower in the morning.

_____

❻ I **leaves** work at 6 o'clock in the evening.

_____

13.12 LISTEN TO THE AUDIO AND ANSWER THE QUESTIONS

Joan talks about her daily routine and work schedule.

She starts work at 4pm.
True ☐ **False** ☑

❶ She finishes work at 12pm.
True ☐ **False** ☐

❷ She eats lunch at 1pm.
True ☐ **False** ☐

❸ She has dinner at 7:30pm.
True ☐ **False** ☐

❹ She watches TV in the afternoon.
True ☐ **False** ☐

❺ She goes on the computer in the evening.
True ☐ **False** ☐

❻ She goes to bed at 8:30pm.
True ☐ **False** ☐

13.13 USE THE CHART TO CREATE 12 CORRECT SENTENCES AND SAY THEM OUT LOUD

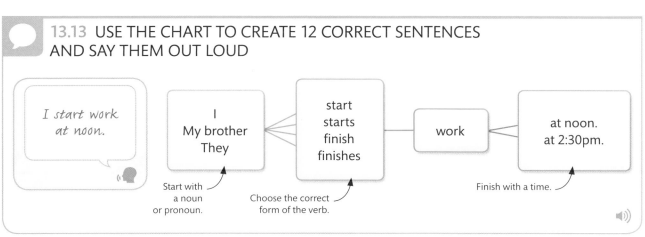

I start work at noon.

| I / My brother / They | start / starts / finish / finishes | work | at noon. / at 2:30pm. |

Start with a noun or pronoun.
Choose the correct form of the verb.
Finish with a time.

13 ✓ CHECKLIST

⚙ The present simple ☐   **Aa** Routine activities ☐   🧩 Talking about your daily routine ☐

49

14 Describing your week

You can talk about your usual weekly activities using the present simple with time phrases. Time phrases are often formed using prepositions and days of the week.

⚙ **New language** Days and prepositions
Aa Vocabulary Days of the week
🧩 **New skill** Talking about your weekly routine

14.1 VOCABULARY DAYS OF THE WEEK

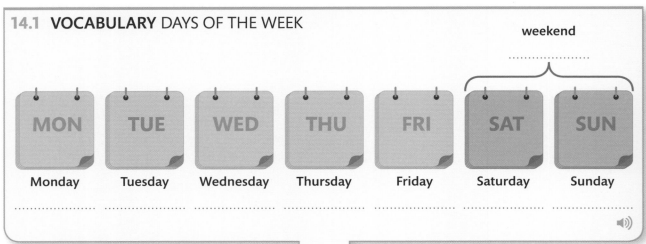

weekend

MON	TUE	WED	THU	FRI	SAT	SUN
Monday	Tuesday	Wednesday	Thursday	Friday	Saturday	Sunday

14.2 KEY LANGUAGE PREPOSITIONS AND DAYS OF THE WEEK

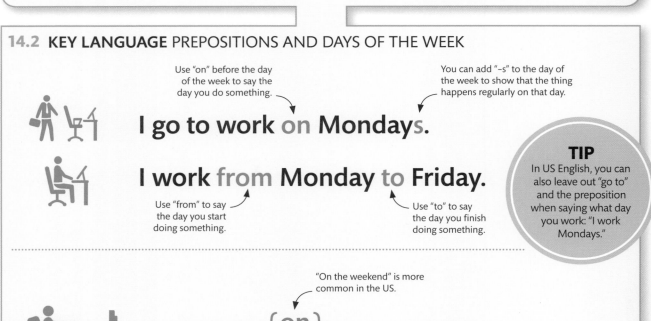

Use "on" before the day of the week to say the day you do something.

You can add "-s" to the day of the week to show that the thing happens regularly on that day.

I go to work on Mondays.

I work from Monday to Friday.

Use "from" to say the day you start doing something.

Use "to" to say the day you finish doing something.

TIP
In US English, you can also leave out "go to" and the preposition when saying what day you work: "I work Mondays."

"On the weekend" is more common in the US.

I watch TV { on / at } the weekend.

"At the weekend" is more common in the UK.

14.3 FILL IN THE GAPS TO COMPLETE THE SENTENCES

Sharon wakes up at 5am __*on*__ Mondays.

1 We eat lunch at 3pm _____ the weekend.

2 She goes to bed at 1am _____ the weekend.

3 I go to work _____ Monday _____ Wednesday.

4 They eat dinner at 9pm _____ the weekend.

5 We finish work at 3pm _____ Fridays.

6 I eat breakfast at work _____ Mondays.

14.4 **VOCABULARY** ACTIVITIES

go to the gym

go swimming

play tennis

play soccer

read the newspaper

take a bath

14.5 FILL IN THE GAPS TO COMPLETE THE SENTENCES

 She __*plays tennis*__ on Mondays.

1 He _____ on Tuesdays and Fridays.

2 They _____ on Thursdays.

3 He _____ on Wednesdays.

4 I _____ on the weekend.

5 You _____ on Saturdays.

14.6 SAY THE SENTENCES OUT LOUD, FILLING IN THE GAPS

I play tennis __*on*__ Wednesdays.

1 I watch TV _____ Sundays.

2 I take a bath _____ 7pm every day.

3 I go to bed _____ 10 o'clock _____ Sundays.

4 I get up _____ 8am _____ Monday to Friday.

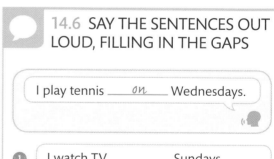

14.7 VOCABULARY FREQUENCY PHRASES

Use frequency phrases to say how often something normally happens.

once a week   **twice a week**   **three times a week**   **every day**

14.8 HOW TO FORM USING FREQUENCY PHRASES

The frequency phrase usually goes at the end of the sentence.

PRESENT SIMPLE	FREQUENCY
I go to the gym	**twice a week.**

14.9 FURTHER EXAMPLES FREQUENCY PHRASES

He goes to work three times a week.

She goes swimming four times a week.

We eat dinner at 7:30pm every day.

They watch TV five times a week.

14.10 LISTEN TO THE AUDIO AND ANSWER THE QUESTIONS

Angela wakes up at 5:30am every day.
True ☐   False ☑

1. Fred works from 8am to 6pm five times a week.
True ☐   False ☐

2. Scott has dinner at 6am.
True ☐   False ☐

3. Linda has a shower every morning.
True ☐   False ☐

4. Jennifer watches TV on the weekend.
True ☐   False ☐

5. Tim's daughter goes to bed at 7:30pm on Sundays.
True ☐   False ☐

14.11 PUT THE WORDS IN ORDER TO FORM A CORRECT SENTENCE

every | day. | a shower | has | He

He has a shower every day.

1. get up | five days | I | at 6am | a week.

2. every | day. | They | at 11pm | go to bed

3. plays | soccer | Sarah | twice a week.

4. once | his clothes | a week. | washes | Jamie

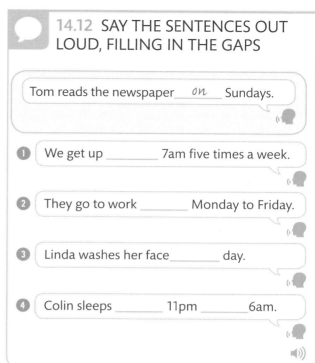

14.12 SAY THE SENTENCES OUT LOUD, FILLING IN THE GAPS

Tom reads the newspaper __on__ Sundays.

1. We get up _____ 7am five times a week.

2. They go to work _____ Monday to Friday.

3. Linda washes her face _____ day.

4. Colin sleeps _____ 11pm _____ 6am.

14 ✓ CHECKLIST

⚙ Days and prepositions ☐   **Aa** Days of the week ☐   🧩 Talking about your weekly routine ☐

↻ REVIEW THE ENGLISH YOU HAVE LEARNED IN UNITS 10-14

NEW LANGUAGE	SAMPLE SENTENCE	☑	UNIT
TALKING ABOUT JOBS	I am **a police officer.** He is **an engineer.**	☐	10.1
USING "WORK IN," "WORK ON," AND "WORK WITH"	I work in **a hospital.** I work on **a farm.** I work with **animals.**	☐	10.8, 10.11
TELLING THE TIME	It's **five.** It's **five o'clock.**	☐	11.1, 11.2
THE PRESENT SIMPLE	I eat **lunch at noon every day.** She eats **lunch at 2pm every day.**	☐	13.1
PREPOSITIONS AND DAYS OF THE WEEK	I work **on Mondays.** I work **from Monday to Friday.**	☐	14.2
FREQUENCY PHRASES	I go to the gym **twice a week.**	☐	14.8, 14.9

15 Negatives with "to be"

You make a sentence negative by using "not" or its short form "n't." Negative sentences with the verb "to be" have different rules than negatives with other verbs.

⚙ **New language** Negatives with "to be"
Aa Vocabulary "Not"
🧩 **New skill** Saying what things are not

15.1 KEY LANGUAGE NEGATIVES WITH THE VERB "TO BE"

Add "not" after "to be" to make the sentence negative.

I am **a farmer**. I am **not a doctor**.

"Not" is added to make the sentence negative.

🔊

15.2 FURTHER EXAMPLES NEGATIVES WITH THE VERB "TO BE"

 He is not **an adult**.

 It is not **5 o'clock**.

 They are not **engineers**.

 This is not **a pig**.

 We are not **actors**.

 That is not **my bag**.

🔊

15.3 HOW TO FORM NEGATIVES WITH THE VERB "TO BE"

The verb "to be" takes the same form in positive and negative sentences. The only difference is adding "not."

SUBJECT + VERB	"NOT"	REST OF SENTENCE
I am She is We are	not	a doctor. doctors.

A plural subject is usually followed by a plural noun.

15.4 REWRITE THE SENTENCES, PUTTING THE WORDS IN THE CORRECT ORDER

gardener. | Jack | not | is | a

Jack is not a gardener.

3 years | I | old. | not | am | 35

_____

1 sister. | my | She | not | is

4 are | not | Spanish. | We

_____

2 her | not | car. | is | That

5 vet. | Chad | a | not | is

_____

🔊

15.5 FILL IN THE GAPS TO MAKE NEGATIVE SENTENCES

It _____ *is not* _____ 11 o'clock.

1 He _____ in the office.

2 She _____ a businesswoman.

3 I _____ 18 years old.

4 This _____ a snake.

5 We _____ artists.

6 You _____ at work.

7 Dexter _____ a cat.

🔊

15.6 LISTEN TO THE AUDIO, THEN NUMBER THE IMAGES IN THE ORDER THEY ARE DESCRIBED

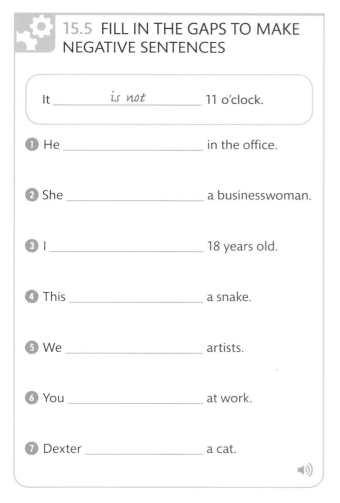

15.7 KEY LANGUAGE NEGATIVE SHORT FORMS

You can contract "you are not" in two ways. You can contract the subject and verb, or you can contract the verb and "not."

"You are" contracts to "you're."

You are not a doctor.

You're not
You aren't } a doctor.

"Are not" contracts to "aren't."

15.8 FURTHER EXAMPLES NEGATIVE SHORT FORMS

I am not a teacher.

I'm not a teacher.
You cannot say "I amn't."

He is not a farmer.

He's not
He isn't } a farmer.

She is not American.

She's not
She isn't } American.

It is not a pencil.

It's not
It isn't } a pencil.

We are not waiters.

We're not
We aren't } waiters.

They are not British.

They're not
They aren't } British.

15.9 REWRITE THE SENTENCES, CORRECTING THE ERRORS

Louis aren't Hayley's uncle.
Louis isn't Hayley's uncle.

❶ It am not 10 o'clock in the morning.

_____

❷ You isn't 35 years old.

_____

❸ I aren't Australian.

_____

❹ My brother aren't married.

_____

❺ Tom and Angela isn't construction workers.

_____

15.10 READ THE BLOG AND ANSWER THE QUESTIONS

Françoise is 33 years old.
True ☐ **False** ☑

① She isn't from the USA.
True ☐ **False** ☐

② She speaks French.
True ☐ **False** ☐

③ She is French.
True ☐ **False** ☐

④ Her husband speaks English.
True ☐ **False** ☐

⑤ Her husband is British.
True ☐ **False** ☐

⑥ They live in the USA.
True ☐ **False** ☐

⑦ Her husband isn't a student.
True ☐ **False** ☐

My life Blog

HOME | ENTRIES | ABOUT | CONTACT

POSTED TUESDAY, OCTOBER 16
ABOUT ME

My name is Françoise, and I'm 35 years old. I speak French, but I'm not from France. I'm from Québec. I'm married to a man called Henry. He speaks English, but he isn't from North America and he isn't from Britain. He's from New Zealand. We don't live in Québec or New Zealand. We live in Ohio, USA. We are graduate students there.

15.11 USE THE CHART TO CREATE 12 CORRECT SENTENCES AND SAY THEM OUT LOUD

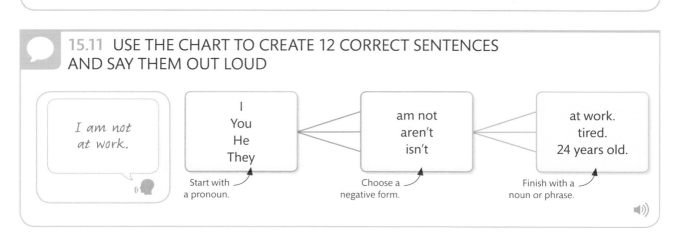

I am not at work.

| I / You / He / They | am not / aren't / isn't | at work. / tired. / 24 years old. |

Start with a pronoun.

Choose a negative form.

Finish with a noun or phrase.

15 ✓ CHECKLIST

⚙ Negatives with "to be" ☐　　**Aa** "Not" ☐　　🧩 Saying what things are not ☐

16 More negatives

Add "do not" or "does not" before most verbs in English to make them negative. This is often shortened to "don't" or "doesn't."

New language Present simple negative
Aa Vocabulary Daily activities
New skill Saying what you don't do

16.1 KEY LANGUAGE PRESENT SIMPLE NEGATIVE

Put "do not" before the verb to make the negative for "I," "you," "we," or "they." After "he," "she," or "it," use "does not."

I work **outside.**

⬇ The main verb does not change.

I **do not** work **outside.**
I work **inside.**

He works **inside.**

⬇

He **does not** work **inside.**
He works **outside.**

16.2 FURTHER EXAMPLES PRESENT SIMPLE NEGATIVE

 You **do not have** a laptop.

 We **do not start** work at 8am.

 He **does not live** in Los Angeles.

 The house **does not have** a backyard.

16.3 HOW TO FORM PRESENT SIMPLE NEGATIVE

Use "do" or "does" with "not" followed by the base form of the main verb (the infinitive without "to").

SUBJECT	"DO / DOES" + "NOT"	BASE FORM	REST OF SENTENCE
I / You / We / They	do not	work	outside.
He / She / It	does not		

16.4 FILL IN THE GAPS USING "DO NOT" OR "DOES NOT"

She _does not_ go to the gym on Thursdays.

1 I _____ read the papers on Saturday.

2 The dog _____ eat fish.

3 They _____ go to the theater often.

4 Ben and I _____ live on a farm now.

5 Theo _____ cycle to work.

6 You _____ work at Fabio's café.

7 Claire _____ watch TV in the evening.

8 We _____ play football at home.

9 Pierre _____ wake up before noon.

16.5 LISTEN TO THE AUDIO AND ANSWER THE QUESTIONS

Frank talks about his daily and weekly routines.

Frank works in a store on Queen Street.
True ✓ **False** ☐

1 Frank gets up at 5am.
True ☐ **False** ☐

2 Frank has lunch at 1pm every day.
True ☐ **False** ☐

3 Frank goes swimming on Wednesday evening.
True ☐ **False** ☐

4 Frank watches TV every night before bed.
True ☐ **False** ☐

16.6 KEY LANGUAGE CONTRACTED NEGATIVES

In English, "do not" and "does not" are often contracted to "don't" and "doesn't."

I do not work outside.
↓
I don't work outside.

He does not work outside.
↓
He doesn't work outside.

16.7 FURTHER EXAMPLES PRESENT SIMPLE NEGATIVE: SHORT FORMS

You don't play soccer.

We don't want that cake.

She doesn't speak English.

He doesn't live near here.

16.8 FILL IN THE GAPS TO WRITE EACH SENTENCE THREE DIFFERENT WAYS

I get up at 7am.	I do not get up at 7am.	I don't get up at 7am.
❶ _____	_____	We don't go to work every day.
❷ _____	He does not watch TV in the evening.	_____
❸ You work in an office.	_____	_____
❹ _____	_____	They don't play tennis.
❺ _____	She does not work with children.	_____

16.9 REWRITE THE SENTENCES, CORRECTING THE ERRORS

He **don't** play soccer on Saturdays.
He *doesn't play soccer on Saturdays.*

❶ We **doesn't** work with animals.

_____

❷ I **doesn't** eat chocolate.

_____

❸ Sandy **don't** work in a hairdresser's.

_____

❹ Melanie and Cris **doesn't** have a car.

_____

❺ They **doesn't** live in Park Road now.

_____

❻ We **doesn't** watch Hollywood movies.

_____

❼ She **don't** drive a taxi.

_____

16.10 USE THE CHART TO CREATE 12 CORRECT SENTENCES AND SAY THEM OUT LOUD

I don't work outside.

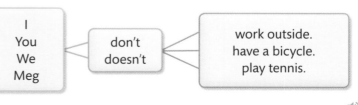

I You We Meg	don't doesn't	work outside. have a bicycle. play tennis.

16.11 READ THE ARTICLE AND ANSWER THE QUESTIONS

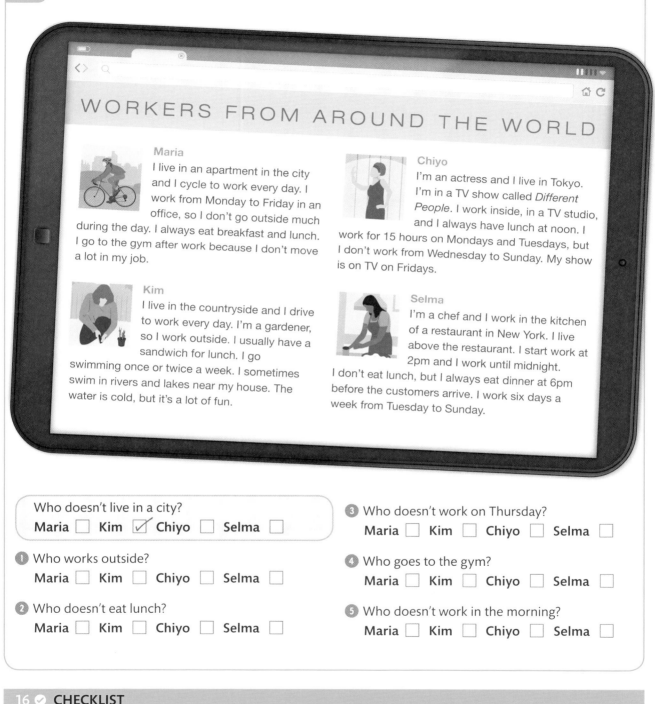

WORKERS FROM AROUND THE WORLD

Maria
I live in an apartment in the city and I cycle to work every day. I work from Monday to Friday in an office, so I don't go outside much during the day. I always eat breakfast and lunch. I go to the gym after work because I don't move a lot in my job.

Chiyo
I'm an actress and I live in Tokyo. I'm in a TV show called *Different People*. I work inside, in a TV studio, and I always have lunch at noon. I work for 15 hours on Mondays and Tuesdays, but I don't work from Wednesday to Sunday. My show is on TV on Fridays.

Kim
I live in the countryside and I drive to work every day. I'm a gardener, so I work outside. I usually have a sandwich for lunch. I go swimming once or twice a week. I sometimes swim in rivers and lakes near my house. The water is cold, but it's a lot of fun.

Selma
I'm a chef and I work in the kitchen of a restaurant in New York. I live above the restaurant. I start work at 2pm and I work until midnight. I don't eat lunch, but I always eat dinner at 6pm before the customers arrive. I work six days a week from Tuesday to Sunday.

Who doesn't live in a city?
Maria ☐ **Kim** ☐ **Chiyo** ☑ **Selma** ☐

❶ Who works outside?
Maria ☐ **Kim** ☐ **Chiyo** ☐ **Selma** ☐

❷ Who doesn't eat lunch?
Maria ☐ **Kim** ☐ **Chiyo** ☐ **Selma** ☐

❸ Who doesn't work on Thursday?
Maria ☐ **Kim** ☐ **Chiyo** ☐ **Selma** ☐

❹ Who goes to the gym?
Maria ☐ **Kim** ☐ **Chiyo** ☐ **Selma** ☐

❺ Who doesn't work in the morning?
Maria ☐ **Kim** ☐ **Chiyo** ☐ **Selma** ☐

---

16 ✓ CHECKLIST

⚙ Present simple negative ☐   **Aa** Daily activities ☐   🧩 Saying what you don't do ☐

17 Simple questions

To form simple questions with the verb "to be," you change the order of the subject and verb. The answer to a simple question usually starts with "yes" or "no."

⚙ **New language** Simple questions
Aa Vocabulary Jobs and routine activities
🧩 **New skill** Asking simple questions

17.1 KEY LANGUAGE QUESTIONS WITH "TO BE"

To make a question using the verb "to be," put the verb before the subject.

In a statement, the subject comes before the verb.

You are **Canadian.**

Are you **Canadian?**

In a question, the verb moves to the start of the sentence.

The subject comes after the verb.

17.2 FURTHER EXAMPLES QUESTIONS WITH "TO BE"

Is Judi **an actor?**

Are they **engineers?**

Is he **French?**

Are you **a student?**

17.3 HOW TO FORM QUESTIONS WITH "TO BE"

"TO BE"	SUBJECT	REST OF SENTENCE
Am	I	
Are	you / we / they	Canadian?
Is	he / she / it	

17.4 REWRITE THE SENTENCES AS QUESTIONS

She is a gardener.
Is she a gardener?

1 Brad is a nurse.

_____

2 These are my keys.

_____

3 Ruby and Farid are actors.

_____

4 This is his laptop.

_____

5 Valeria is his sister.

_____

17.5 LISTEN TO THE AUDIO AND CIRCLE THE CORRECT ANSWER TO EACH QUESTION

1 **2**

3 **4**

5 **6**

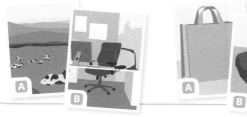

17.6 **INTONATION** SIMPLE QUESTIONS

The tone of the voice usually rises at the end of a simple question in English.

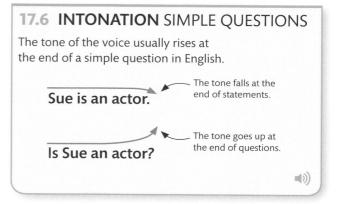

Sue is an actor. The tone falls at the end of statements.

Is Sue an actor? The tone goes up at the end of questions.

17.7 SAY THESE SENTENCES OUT LOUD, FILLING IN THE GAPS

_____*Is*_____ she a waitress?

1 _____ Holly your mother?

2 _____ they from Argentina?

3 _____ you a teacher?

4 _____ this your dog?

5 _____ there a post office?

17.8 KEY LANGUAGE QUESTIONS WITH "DO" AND "DOES"

For questions without the verb "to be," start the question with "do" or "does."

You work in an office.

↓

Do you work in an office?

Add "do" to questions with "I," "you," "we," and "they."

She works in a school.

↓

Does she work in a school?

Add "does" to questions with "he," "she," and "it."

The main verb is in its base form (the infinitive without "to").

17.9 FURTHER EXAMPLES QUESTIONS WITH "DO" AND "DOES"

 Do they live in Paris?

 Does Tom get up at 6am?

 Do you finish work at 4pm today?

 Does the party start at 7pm?

17.10 HOW TO FORM QUESTIONS WITH "DO" AND "DOES"

"DO" / "DOES"	SUBJECT	BASE FORM OF VERB	REST OF SENTENCE
Do	I / you / we / they	work	in an office?
Does	he / she / it		

17.11 FILL IN THE GAPS IN THE QUESTIONS USING "DO" OR "DOES"

 Does she play tennis on Tuesdays?

❸ _____ we finish work at 6pm today?

❶ _____ you get up at 7am?

❹ _____ the parrot talk all day?

❷ _____ they live at number 59?

❺ _____ you work in a lab?

17.12 REWRITE THE QUESTIONS, PUTTING THE WORDS IN THE CORRECT ORDER

go swimming | Jin | Does | on Fridays?

Does Jin go swimming on Fridays?

1 in New York? | live | you | Do

_____

2 on a farm? | Does | work | she

_____

3 get up | he | Does | at 5am | every day?

_____

4 come | Peru? | they | Do | from

_____

5 work | Brad | Does | in the post office?

_____

17.13 REWRITE THE SENTENCES AS QUESTIONS

Kim goes to work at 8am.

Does Kim go to work at 8am?

1 They live in New York City.

_____

2 He works in a restaurant.

_____

3 Lewis goes swimming on Fridays.

_____

4 Marisha works with animals.

_____

17.14 SAY THE SENTENCES OUT LOUD, FILLING IN THE GAPS

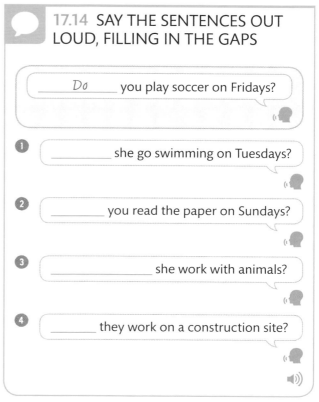

Do you play soccer on Fridays?

1 _____ she go swimming on Tuesdays?

2 _____ you read the paper on Sundays?

3 _____ she work with animals?

4 _____ they work on a construction site?

---

17 ✓ **CHECKLIST**

⚙ Simple questions ☐   **Aa** Jobs and routine activities ☐   🧩 Asking simple questions ☐

18 Answering questions

When answering questions in English, you can often leave out words to shorten your response. These short answers are often used in spoken English.

⚙ **New language** Short answers
Aa Vocabulary Jobs and routines
🧩 **New skill** Answering spoken questions

18.1 KEY LANGUAGE SHORT ANSWERS

When the question uses the verb "to be," use "to be" in the short answer. If the question uses "do" or "does," so does the short answer.

Question uses "to be."

Are you a doctor?

Yes, I am.

No, I'm not.

You don't need to repeat "a doctor" in your answer.

Do you work in an office?

Yes, I do.

No, I don't.

Question uses "do."

The rest of the sentence is implied.

18.2 FURTHER EXAMPLES SHORT ANSWERS

Does he live here?

Yes, he does.

No, he doesn't.

Question uses "does."

Do they live in Delhi?

Yes, they do.

No, they don't.

Is your name Sophie?

Yes, it is.

No, it isn't.

Are you Chinese?

Yes, I am.

No, I'm not.

18.3 LISTEN TO THE AUDIO AND ANSWER THE QUESTIONS

Maria Kowalski goes for a job interview.

She is from Poland. **True** ☐ **False** ✓

❶ She is a receptionist. **True** ☐ **False** ☐

❷ She works in an office. **True** ☐ **False** ☐

❸ She doesn't like her job. **True** ☐ **False** ☐

❹ She starts work at 9am. **True** ☐ **False** ☐

❺ She works five days a week. **True** ☐ **False** ☐

18.4 MARK THE CORRECT REPLY TO EACH QUESTION

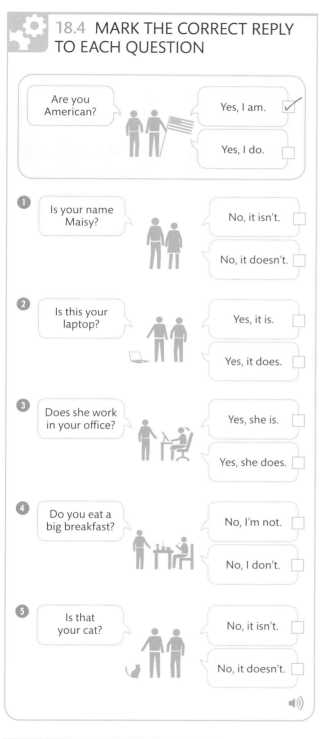

Are you American?

Yes, I am. ✓

Yes, I do.

1 Is your name Maisy?

No, it isn't.

No, it doesn't.

2 Is this your laptop?

Yes, it is.

Yes, it does.

3 Does she work in your office?

Yes, she is.

Yes, she does.

4 Do you eat a big breakfast?

No, I'm not.

No, I don't.

5 Is that your cat?

No, it isn't.

No, it doesn't.

🔊))

18.5 ANSWER THE QUESTIONS, SPEAKING OUT LOUD

Does Joe watch TV?

Yes, _____he does_____. 🗣))

1 Are you a student?

No, _____. 🗣

2 Do they speak English?

Yes, _____. 🗣

3 Is that your house?

No, _____. 🗣

4 Does she play tennis?

Yes, _____. 🗣

5 Is Miranda your aunt?

No, _____. 🗣

6 Do they work in a hospital?

Yes, _____. 🗣

7 Is he your grandfather?

No, _____. 🗣

🔊))

18 ✓ CHECKLIST

⚙ Short answers ☐   **Aa** Jobs and routines ☐   🧩 Answering spoken questions ☐

19 Asking questions

Use question words such as "what," "who," "when," and "where" to ask open questions that can't be answered with "yes" or "no."

🔧 **New language** Open questions
Aa Vocabulary Question words
🧩 **New skill** Asking for details

19.1 KEY LANGUAGE OPEN QUESTIONS WITH THE VERB "TO BE"

The question word goes at the beginning of the question. It is usually followed by the verb "to be."

> **My name is Sarah.**
> **What is your name?**

The question word goes at the beginning.

The question is "open" because it can't be answered "yes" or "no."

19.2 FURTHER EXAMPLES OPEN QUESTIONS WITH THE VERB "TO BE"

What is Ruby's job?

What is the time?

What is in the bag?

What are we here for?

What is this thing?

What are Elliot's sisters called?

19.3 CROSS OUT THE INCORRECT WORDS IN EACH SENTENCE

What is / ~~are~~ / ~~am~~ the capital of France?

1. What is / are / am their names?

2. What is / are / am the time?

3. What is / are / am my favorite colors?

4. What is / are / am the hotel next to?

5. What is / are / am they?

6. What is / are / am your uncle's name?

7. What is / are / am my name?

19.4 VOCABULARY
QUESTION WORDS

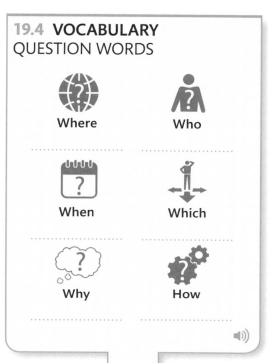

Where

Who

When

Which

Why

How

19.5 FURTHER EXAMPLES
QUESTION WORDS

Where is the café?

Who is Jo's teacher?

When is dinner?

Which is your car?

Why am I here?

How are you?

Aa 19.6 MATCH THE QUESTIONS TO THE CORRECT ANSWERS

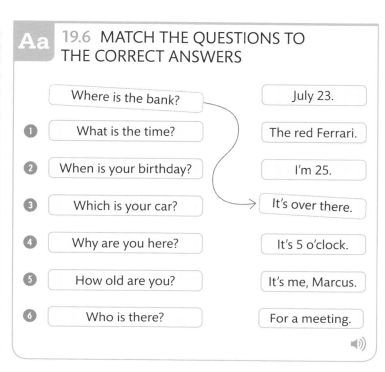

Where is the bank? → It's over there.

1. What is the time? — It's 5 o'clock.

2. When is your birthday? — July 23.

3. Which is your car? — The red Ferrari.

4. Why are you here? — For a meeting.

5. How old are you? — I'm 25.

6. Who is there? — It's me, Marcus.

Answers: July 23. / The red Ferrari. / I'm 25. / It's over there. / It's 5 o'clock. / It's me, Marcus. / For a meeting.

19.7 FILL IN THE GAPS USING THE WORDS IN THE PANEL

What is your name?

1. _____ are your parents from?

2. _____ old are you?

3. _____ is breakfast?

4. _____ is your friend talking to?

5. _____ is it cold in here?

6. _____ person is your teacher?

What   Where   Who   When
Which   Why   How

19.8 KEY LANGUAGE OPEN QUESTIONS USING "DO" AND "DOES"

With most verbs other than "to be" you use the question word followed by "do" or "does" to make a question.

"Do" or "does" follows the question word.

When do you eat lunch?

The question word goes at the beginning.

Main verb changes to its base form.

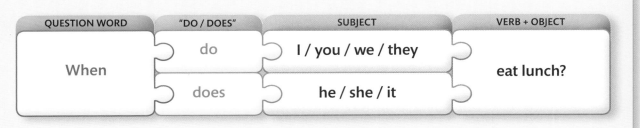

19.9 HOW TO FORM OPEN QUESTIONS USING "DO" AND "DOES"

QUESTION WORD	"DO / DOES"	SUBJECT	VERB + OBJECT
When	do	I / you / we / they	eat lunch?
	does	he / she / it	

19.10 FURTHER EXAMPLES OPEN QUESTIONS USING "DO" AND "DOES"

Where do **you go swimming?**

When does **he finish work?**

What does **she do on the weekend?**

Which car do **you drive to work?**

19.11 FILL IN THE GAPS TO COMPLETE THE QUESTIONS

When _____*do*_____ they start work?

① When _____ she eat lunch?

② Where _____ they live?

③ Which bag _____ you want?

④ Where _____ he come from?

⑤ When _____ the movie end?

19.12 REWRITE THE SENTENCES, PUTTING THE WORDS IN THE CORRECT ORDER

eat | do | When | breakfast? | you

When do you eat breakfast?

1 does | play | he | football? | Where

_____

2 you | When | clean | do | car? | the

_____

3 the | start? | What | party | does | time

_____

4 tennis? | Which | do | days | play | you

_____

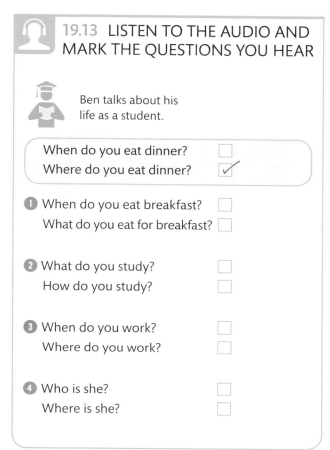

19.13 LISTEN TO THE AUDIO AND MARK THE QUESTIONS YOU HEAR

Ben talks about his life as a student.

When do you eat dinner? ☐
Where do you eat dinner? ✓

1 When do you eat breakfast? ☐
What do you eat for breakfast? ☐

2 What do you study? ☐
How do you study? ☐

3 When do you work? ☐
Where do you work? ☐

4 Who is she? ☐
Where is she? ☐

19.14 SAY THE QUESTIONS OUT LOUD, FILLING IN THE GAPS USING THE WORDS IN THE PANEL

___*What*___ do you do for a living?

1 _____ do you work in the city?

2 _____ do you start work?

3 _____ time does it open?

4 _____ many people do you work with?

5 _____ do you work with?

| When | How | ~~What~~ | What | Where | Who |

19.15 READ THE EMAIL AND ANSWER THE QUESTIONS

Which village is Bernadette in?
Torremolinos ☐
Mijas ☑

❶ Who is Bernadette on vacation with?
Her brother ☐
Her sister ☐

❷ How many swimming pools does the hotel have?
Two ☐
Three ☐

❸ What time does Bernadette get up?
At 7am ☐
At 7:30am ☐

❹ What does Bernadette do in the morning?
Goes to the gym ☐
Goes swimming ☐

❺ Where does Bernadette have breakfast?
In her room ☐
By the pool ☐

❻ When is the flamenco dancing?
Tonight ☐
Tomorrow ☐

✉

To: Mary Jones

Subject: Vacation in Spain

Hi Mary.

We're in Spain, in a village called Mijas, near Torremolinos. My sister is at work this week, so I'm here with my brother, John. Our hotel is next to some apartments. It's in a complex and has two swimming pools and a gym. Breakfast is from 7:30am until 9 every morning, so I get up at 7am and have a swim before I eat. John stays in his room and we meet later for breakfast. The restaurant is by the pool. We have our breakfast there every day. There's also dancing at night. There's salsa dancing tonight, and tomorrow it's flamenco.

See you soon,
Bernadette

19.16 USE THE CHART TO CREATE 12 CORRECT SENTENCES AND SAY THEM OUT LOUD

Where does Kate play golf?

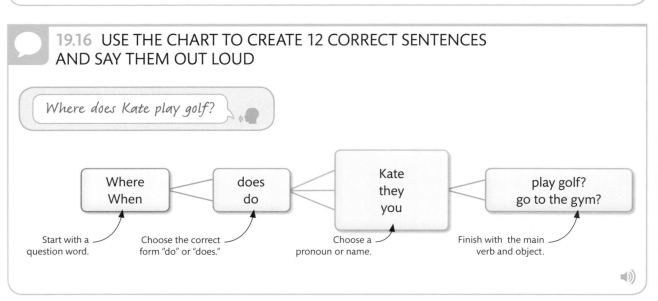

| Where / When | does / do | Kate / they / you | play golf? / go to the gym? |

Start with a question word.

Choose the correct form "do" or "does."

Choose a pronoun or name.

Finish with the main verb and object.

19.17 REWRITE THE SENTENCES, CORRECTING THE ERRORS

> Where are my laptop?
> _Where is my laptop?_

1 How often does they play tennis?

_____

2 Which office do he work in?

_____

3 Where are the party?

_____

4 What does you do?

_____

19.18 FILL IN THE GAPS TO COMPLETE THE QUESTIONS

> When _does Russell go to the gym?_
> Russell goes to the gym on Tuesdays.

1 What _____ ?

Her cat is called Ginger.

2 Who _____ ?

My English teacher is Mrs. Price.

3 Where _____ ?

Ben works in a hospital.

4 How _____ ?

My grandmother is fine, thanks.

---

19 ✓ CHECKLIST

⚙ Open questions ☐   **Aa** Question words ☐   🧩 Asking for details ☐

↻ REVIEW THE ENGLISH YOU HAVE LEARNED IN UNITS 15-19

NEW LANGUAGE	SAMPLE SENTENCE	☑	UNIT
NEGATIVES WITH "TO BE"	I am a farmer. I am not a doctor. You're not a doctor. You aren't a doctor.	☐	15.1, 15.3, 15.7
PRESENT SIMPLE NEGATIVE	He does not work inside. He works outside. I work outside. I do not work inside.	☐	16.1, 16.3, 16.6
SIMPLE QUESTIONS	Are you Canadian? Do you work in an office? Does she work in a school?	☐	17.1, 17.8
SHORT ANSWERS	Are you a doctor? Yes, I am. Do you work in an office? No, I don't.	☐	18.1, 18.2
OPEN QUESTIONS WITH "TO BE"	My name is Sarah. What is your name?	☐	19.1, 19.2
OPEN QUESTIONS USING "DO" AND "DOES"	When do you eat lunch? When does she eat lunch?	☐	19.8, 19.9

20 Vocabulary

20.1 AROUND TOWN

village

town

city

hospital

police station

bus station

bus stop

train station

airport

school

factory

supermarket

store (US)
shop (UK)

pharmacy

bank

post office

library

museum

 town hall

 castle

 office building

 park

 here

 bridge

 swimming pool

 restaurant

 café

 there

 bar

 movie theater (US) cinema (UK)

 theater (US) theatre (UK)

 hotel

 near

 church

 mosque

 synagogue

 temple

 far

21 Talking about your town

When you talk about things, you can use "there is" for one and "there are" for more than one. "There isn't" and "there aren't" are the negatives.

⚙ **New language** "There is" and "there are"
Aa Vocabulary Towns and buildings
🧩 **New skill** Describing a town

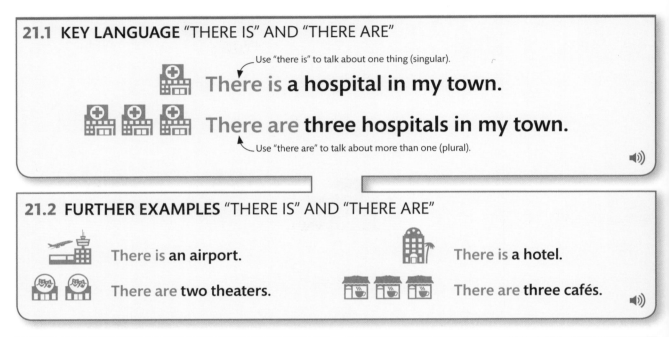

21.1 KEY LANGUAGE "THERE IS" AND "THERE ARE"

Use "there is" to talk about one thing (singular).

There is a hospital in my town.

There are three hospitals in my town.

Use "there are" to talk about more than one (plural).

21.2 FURTHER EXAMPLES "THERE IS" AND "THERE ARE"

There is **an airport.**

There are **two theaters.**

There is **a hotel.**

There are **three cafés.**

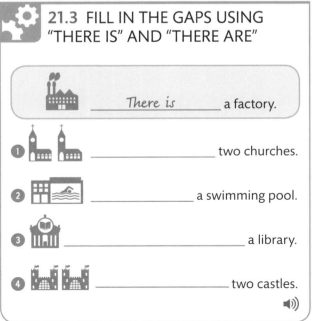

21.3 FILL IN THE GAPS USING "THERE IS" AND "THERE ARE"

There is a factory.

1 _____ two churches.

2 _____ a swimming pool.

3 _____ a library.

4 _____ two castles.

21.4 SAY THESE PLURALS OUT LOUD

libraries

1 airports

2 theaters

3 schools

4 hospitals

5 bars

6 churches

7 factories

8 offices

Aa 21.5 LOOK AT THE PICTURES AND FILL IN THE GAPS TO COMPLETE THE SENTENCES

There is a _town hall_ .

1 There are _____ .

2 There are _____ .

3 There is a _____ .

4 There is a _____ .

5 There are _____ .

21.6 KEY LANGUAGE "THERE IS NOT" AND "THERE ARE NOT ANY"

Add "not" to make a singular sentence negative.

There is **not a school.**

There is**n't a school.**

You can shorten "is not" to "isn't."

Add "not any" to make a plural sentence negative.

There are **not any schools.**

There are**n't any schools.**

You can shorten "are not" to "aren't."

21.7 CROSS OUT THE INCORRECT WORD IN EACH SENTENCE

There isn't / ~~aren't~~ a castle.

1 There isn't / aren't a theater.

2 There isn't / aren't any factories.

3 There isn't / aren't a bus station.

4 There isn't / aren't any airports.

5 There isn't / aren't any churches.

21.8 ANOTHER WAY TO SAY "THERE AREN'T ANY"

You can use "are no" instead of "aren't any." It means the same thing.

This is the contracted form of "are not."

There aren't any **stores.**

There are no **stores.**

21.9 FURTHER EXAMPLES "ARE NO"

There are no **libraries in Oldtown.**

There are no **factories in Newport.**

There are no **schools in our village.**

21.10 FILL IN THE GAPS USING "ARE" AND "AREN'T"

There ___*aren't*___ any theaters.

1 There _____ no castles.

2 There _____ any factories.

3 There _____ no hospitals.

4 There _____ any churches.

5 There _____ no swimming pools.

6 There _____ no airports.

21.11 LISTEN TO THE AUDIO, THEN NUMBER THE PICTURES IN THE ORDER THEY ARE DESCRIBED

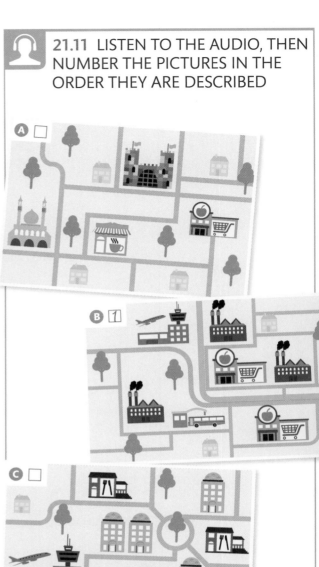

A ☐

B 1

C ☐

D ☐

21.12 READ THE EMAIL AND ANSWER THE QUESTIONS

There are two schools.
True ☐ **False** ☑

1 There is a supermarket.
True ☐ **False** ☐

2 There is a theater.
True ☐ **False** ☐

3 There are four movie theaters.
True ☐ **False** ☐

4 There are three restaurants.
True ☐ **False** ☐

✉

To: Matt

Subject: Our new place

Hi Matt,
We're in our new house in Littleton and it's great! There are three schools in the town, so that's good for the children. There's also a big swimming pool and Joanne goes there every evening. I work in an office above the supermarket. It's near our house.
There are lots of things to do on the weekend. There isn't a theater, but there are two movie theaters, three restaurants, and a library. There's also a great museum. We go there every weekend because the children love it!
Come and see us soon. It's easy to get here. There isn't an airport or a train station, but there's a bus station.
See you soon! Jamal

21.13 LOOK AT THE PICTURE, THEN SAY EACH SENTENCE OUT LOUD, FILLING IN THE GAPS

There is a supermarket.

1 _____ a park.

2 _____ a hotel.

3 _____ no cafés.

4 _____ an airport.

5 _____ stores.

6 _____ a train station.

7 _____ theaters.

21 ✓ CHECKLIST

⚙ "There is" and "there are" ☐   **Aa** Towns and buildings ☐   🧩 Describing a town ☐

22 Using "a" and "the"

Use the definite article ("the") or indefinite article
("a," "an") to talk about things in specific or general
terms. Use "some" to talk about more than one thing.

⚙ **New language** Definite and indefinite articles
Aa Vocabulary Places in town
🧩 **New skill** Using articles

22.1 KEY LANGUAGE "A / AN / THE"

Use "a" to talk
about a thing
in general. Use
"the" to talk about
a place, person,
or thing that you
and the listener
both know about.

Use "a" because you are talking about your work
in general, not the specific place where you work.

I work in a library.

I work in the library on Main Street.

Use "the" because you are talking about
the specific building where you work.

22.2 FURTHER EXAMPLES "A / AN / THE"

Use "a / an" to talk about jobs.

Jim is an artist.

Use "an" before words
that start with a vowel.

Is there a bank near here?

Use "a" with "is there"
and "there is."

Use "the" to talk about a particular doctor.

The doctor at my hospital is good.

I go to the bank on Broad Street.

Use "the" to talk about a particular bank.

⚙ 22.3 CROSS OUT THE INCORRECT WORDS IN EACH SENTENCE

Charlotte is ~~a~~ / an / ~~the~~ actress.

1 A / An / The new teacher is called Miss Jones.

2 There is a / an / the good café in the park.

3 I work at a / an / the hotel next to the library.

4 There is a / an / the swimming pool near my office.

5 It is a / an / the dog's favorite toy.

6 Janie is a / an / the artist at the gallery.

7 See you at a / an / the café at the bus station.

22.4 KEY LANGUAGE "A / SOME"

You can only use "a" and "an" for singular nouns. Use "some" for plurals.

Use "a" and "an" to talk about one thing.

Singular.

There is a hotel in the town.

There are some hotels in the town.

Use "some" to talk about more than one thing.

Plural.

22.5 FURTHER EXAMPLES "A / SOME"

There is a bank on Main Street.

There are some banks on Main Street.

There is a waiter over there.

There are some children in the park.

22.6 FILL IN THE GAPS WITH "A" OR "SOME"

There is _____*a*_____ restaurant in the park.

1 There are _____ stores on Broad Street.

2 There is _____ café next to the castle.

3 There are _____ cakes on the table.

4 There is _____ phone here.

5 There are _____ factories downtown.

22.7 REWRITE THE SENTENCES, CORRECTING THE ERRORS

There **are** a movie theater on Main Street.
There is a movie theater on Main Street.

1 There **is** some supermarkets in town.

_____

2 There **are** an office near the river.

_____

3 There **is** some chocolate bars in my bag.

_____

4 There **are** a hospital near the bus station.

_____

22.8 KEY LANGUAGE QUESTIONS WITH "A / ANY"

There is a hotel in the town.

Is there a hotel in the town?

Use "a" to find out if there is one of something.

There are some hotels in the town.

Are there any hotels in the town?

Use "any" to find out if there is one or more of something.

22.9 FURTHER EXAMPLES QUESTIONS WITH "A / ANY"

Is there a restaurant?

Is there a hospital?

Are there any factories?

Are there any theaters?

22.10 CROSS OUT THE INCORRECT WORDS IN EACH QUESTION

Is there a / ~~an~~ / ~~any~~ hospital in the town?

1 Are there a / an / any stores on your street?

2 Is there a / an / any airport near Littleton?

3 Are there a / an / any mosques in the city?

4 Is there a / an / any swimming pool downtown?

5 Are there a / an / any offices in that building?

22.11 REWRITE THE SENTENCES, PUTTING THE WORDS IN THE CORRECT ORDER

| any | in | town? | Are | your | factories | there |

Are there any factories in your town?

1 | there | here? | a | Is | supermarket | near |

2 | on | there | any | Elm Road? | Are | cafés |

3 | Are | your house? | there | any | near | hotels |

4 | a | café | office? | there | near | Is | your |

5 | the | there | a bar | next to | Is | bank? |

22.12 KEY LANGUAGE SHORT ANSWERS

When answering questions in English, you don't have to repeat all the words from the question.

Short for: "Yes, there is a hotel in the town."

Is there a hotel in the town?

Yes, there is.

No, there isn't.

Are there any hotels in the town?

Yes, there are.

No, there aren't.

Short for: "No, there aren't any hotels in the town."

22.13 FILL IN THE GAPS WITH SHORT ANSWERS

Are there any theaters in Littleton?
No, _there aren't_ .

1 Is there a church on Main Street?
Yes, _____.

2 Are there any pens in your bag?
Yes, _____.

3 Is there a post office near here?
No, _____.

4 Are there any supermarkets on Station Road?
Yes, _____.

5 Is there a school near your house?
No, _____.

6 Are there any dogs in the hotel?
No, _____.

22.14 LOOK AT THE MAP AND ANSWER THE QUESTIONS, SPEAKING OUT LOUD

Is there a library? | Yes, there is.

1 Are there any hotels?

2 Is there a church?

3 Are there two cafés?

4 Is there a supermarket?

22 ✓ CHECKLIST

⚙ Definite and indefinite articles ☐   **Aa** Places in town ☐   🧩 Using articles ☐

23 Orders and directions

Use imperatives to tell someone to do something. They are also useful to give a warning, or to give directions to someone.

⚙ **New language** Imperatives
Aa Vocabulary Directions
🧩 **New skill** Finding your way

23.1 KEY LANGUAGE IMPERATIVES

To make the imperative, use the base form of the verb (the infinitive without "to").

Stop!

The base form of the verb "to stop."

23.2 FURTHER EXAMPLES IMPERATIVES

 Get up.

 Eat your breakfast.

 Give that to me.

 Be careful!

 Help!

 Read this book.

23.3 REWRITE THE INFINITIVES AS IMPERATIVES

| to go | = | *Go* |

① to wake up = _____

② to do = _____

③ to start = _____

④ to have = _____

⑤ to wait = _____

⑥ to stop = _____

⑦ to work = _____

23.4 KEY LANGUAGE
GIVING DIRECTIONS

go straight ahead

turn left

turn right

go past

take the first right

take the second right

23.5 MARK THE DIRECTIONS THAT LEAD YOU TO THE CORRECT PLACES ON THE MAP

You are here

For the Bridge Café:
Take the first right. The café is on the left. ☑
Take the first left. The café is on the right. ☐

1 For the train station:
Take the second left. The station is on the right. ☐
Take the second right. The station is on the left. ☐

2 For the Elm Tree Restaurant:
Take the first left, then turn right. The restaurant is on the right. ☐
Take the second left, then turn right. The restaurant is on the left. ☐

3 For the hospital:
Take the second right, and the hospital is on the left. ☐
Take the second left, and the hospital is on the right. ☐

4 For the Supreme Hotel:
Take the first left, then go straight ahead. The hotel is on the right. ☐
Take the first right, then go straight ahead. The hotel is on the left. ☐

5 For the castle:
Take the first left, then turn right. The castle is on the left. ☐
Take the first left, then turn left. The castle is on the right. ☐

23.6 VOCABULARY DIRECTIONS

next to
....

opposite
....

between
....

on the corner
....

behind
....

in front of
....

on the right
....

on the left
....

intersection (US)
crossroads (UK)
....

block
....

Aa 23.7 FILL IN THE GAPS USING DIRECTIONS

The Rathbone Theater is
_____*opposite*_____ the park.

❶ The supermarket is
_____ the post office.

❷ The museum is
_____ the café.

❸ The station is
_____ the church.

❹ The cinema is on the
_____ of the intersection.

❺ The post office is_____
the café and the supermarket.

23.8 KEY LANGUAGE NEGATIVE IMPERATIVE

Add "don't" or "do not" before the verb to make an imperative negative.

Do not
Don't
} turn right.

🔊

23.9 FURTHER EXAMPLES NEGATIVE IMPERATIVE

Don't eat **that cake.**

Don't sit **there.**

🔊

23.10 REWRITE THE SENTENCES AS NEGATIVE IMPERATIVES

Take the first left.
Don't take the first left.

① Read that book.

_____

② Go past the hotel.

_____

③ Give that to the cat.

_____

④ Have a shower.

_____

⑤ Drive to the mall.

_____

🔊

23.11 LISTEN AND MATCH THE DIRECTIONS TO THE PLACES

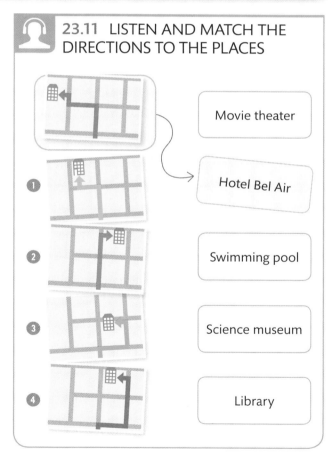

Movie theater

Hotel Bel Air

Swimming pool

Science museum

Library

23 ✓ CHECKLIST

⚙ Imperatives ☐   **Aa** Directions ☐   🧩 Finding your way ☐

24 Joining sentences

"And" and "but" are conjunctions: words that join statements together. "And" adds things to a sentence or links sentences together. "But" introduces a contrast to a sentence.

⚙ **New language** Using "and" and "but"
Aa Vocabulary Town, jobs, and family
🧩 **New skill** Joining sentences

24.1 KEY LANGUAGE USING "AND" TO JOIN SENTENCES

Use "and" to join two sentences together.

"There's" is the same as "There is."

There's a library. There's a restaurant.

⬇

There's a library and a restaurant.

You can drop the second "there's" when you join sentences using "and."

🔊

24.2 FURTHER EXAMPLES USING "AND" TO JOIN SENTENCES

Jazmin's sister lives and works in Paris.

My father and brother are both engineers.

Simon plays video games and watches TV every night.

🔊

24.3 REWRITE THESE STATEMENTS AS SINGLE SENTENCES USING "AND"

I get up. I have a shower.
I get up and have a shower.

① There are two hotels. There are three shops.

_____

② Hilda works in a school. She works in a theater.

_____

③ My uncle is a scientist. My aunt is a doctor.

_____

④ Sue watches TV. She reads books.

_____

⑤ The store opens at night. Jan starts work.

_____

🔊

24.4 LISTEN TO THE AUDIO AND MATCH THE PLACES MENTIONED IN EACH "AND" STATEMENT

 **1**

 **2**

 **3**

 **4**

A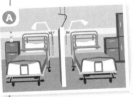

B

C

D

E

24.5 KEY LANGUAGE USING A COMMA INSTEAD OF "AND"

For lists of more than two items, you can use commas instead of "and."

You can use a comma to replace "and" in a list.

Use another comma before the "and."

There's a library, a store, and a café.

Keep the "and" between the final two nouns.

24.6 MARK THE SENTENCES THAT USE COMMAS AND "AND" CORRECTLY

I am a wife, a mother, and a daughter. ☑
I am a wife, and a mother, a daughter. ☐

1 There are hotels and bars and stores. ☐
There are hotels, bars, and stores. ☐

2 Sam eats, breakfast lunch and dinner. ☐
Sam eats breakfast, lunch, and dinner. ☐

3 I play tennis, soccer, and chess. ☐
I play tennis, and soccer, and chess. ☐

4 Teo plays with his car and his train and his bus. ☐
Teo plays with his car, train, and bus. ☐

5 There is a pencil, a bag and, a cell phone. ☐
There is a pencil, a bag, and a cell phone. ☐

6 My friends, girlfriend, and aunt are here. ☐
My friends, and, girlfriend and aunt are here. ☐

7 Ling works on Monday, Thursday, and Friday. ☐
Ling works on Monday, and Thursday, Friday. ☐

24.7 KEY LANGUAGE USING "BUT" TO JOIN SENTENCES

Use "but" to join a positive and a negative statement.

There's a hotel. There isn't a store.

There's a hotel, but there isn't a store.

You can use "but" to add something negative to a positive sentence.

There isn't a store here, but there is a hotel.

You can use "but" to add something positive to a negative sentence.

24.8 MATCH THE BEGINNINGS OF THE SENTENCES TO THE CORRECT ENDINGS

There is a mosque, but —————————→ there isn't a church.

① This is my car, but — these aren't my car keys.

② We eat a small breakfast, but — it doesn't have a bathtub.

③ I work from Monday to Friday, but — not on the weekend.

④ The bathroom has a shower, but — we eat a big lunch.

24.9 REWRITE EACH PAIR OF STATEMENTS AS A SINGLE SENTENCE

There is a post office. There isn't a bank.
There is a post office, but there isn't a bank.

① There isn't a bathtub. There is a shower.

_____

② There isn't a bar. There is a café.

_____

③ This bag is Maya's. That laptop isn't hers.

_____

④ Si doesn't have any dogs. He has two cats.

_____

⑤ Sally reads books. She never watches TV.

_____

24.10 CROSS OUT THE INCORRECT WORD IN EACH SENTENCE

I am a father and / ~~but~~ a son.

 1 Lu reads books and / but magazines.

2 I work every weekday, and / but not on weekends.

3 Jim is a husband and / but a father.

4 There is a cinema, and / but no theater.

5 There isn't a gym, and / but there is a pool.

🔊

24.11 LOOK AT THE TABLE, THEN SAY "AND" AND "BUT" SENTENCES OUT LOUD

✓	✓	✗

There is ___a mosque and a church,___ ___but there isn't a factory___ .

1 There is _____ .

2 There is _____ .

3 There is _____ .

4 There is _____ .

🔊

24 ✓ CHECKLIST

⚙ Using "and" and "but" ☐   **Aa** Town, jobs, and family ☐   🧩 Joining sentences ☐

91

25 Describing places

Use adjectives to give more information about nouns, for example to describe a person, building, or place.

✿ **New language** Adjectives
Aa Vocabulary Place adjectives and nouns
🧩 **New skill** Describing places

25.1 KEY LANGUAGE USING ADJECTIVES

Adjectives are usually placed before the noun they describe.

She is a busy woman.

He is a busy man.

⤷ Adjectives are the same for male and female nouns.

It is a busy town.

These are busy streets.

⤷ Adjectives are the same for singular and plural nouns.

🔊

25.2 VOCABULARY ADJECTIVES

old

....

new

....

beautiful

....

horrible

....

busy

....

quiet

....

small

....

big

....

🔊

25.3 REWRITE THE SENTENCES, PUTTING THE WORDS IN THE CORRECT ORDER

| a | This | is | town. | beautiful |

This is a beautiful town.

1 | horrible | is | He | man. | a |

_____

2 | are | They | small | children. |

_____

3 | uncle | My | man. | is | a quiet |

_____

4 | large | is | There | a | cake. |

_____

5 | my | shoes. | are | old | These |

_____

6 | supermarket. | a | new | is | There |

_____

7 | in | work | You | museum. | an old |

_____

◀))

25.4 OTHER WAYS TO USE ADJECTIVES

Sometimes, adjectives can be put
in different places in a sentence.

The town is busy.

You can put the adjective at the end of
the sentence after the verb "to be."

Southbay is a busy town.

The adjective usually
comes before the noun.

It is busy.

You can replace the
noun with a pronoun.

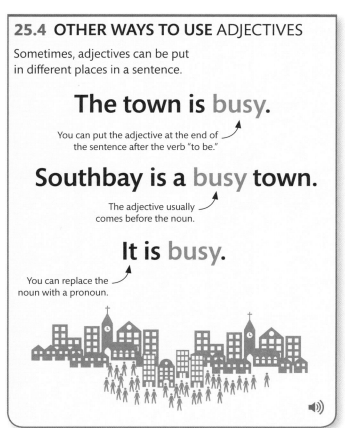

◀))

Aa 25.5 READ THE PASSAGE AND CIRCLE SEVEN ADJECTIVES

Hi! I'm Paolo.

I live and work in a (small) town.
There are some beautiful old buildings
there and lots of hotels, too. I work
in a large restaurant near the river.
I'm a waiter and my friend is the chef.
The restaurant is busy every evening
and my job is horrible, but the food
is beautiful. I eat there every day.

25.6 FILL IN THE GAPS TO WRITE EACH SENTENCE THREE DIFFERENT WAYS

| Rome is an **old** city. | _The city is old._ | _It is old._ |

① She is a **busy** nurse.

② He is a **quiet** dog.

③ They are **new** patients.

④ It is a **horrible** town.

⑤ It is a **beautiful** car.

25.7 **VOCABULARY** PLACES AND SCENERY

beach

sea

sand

grass

countryside

tree

hill

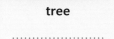
river

mountain

lake

sky

cloud

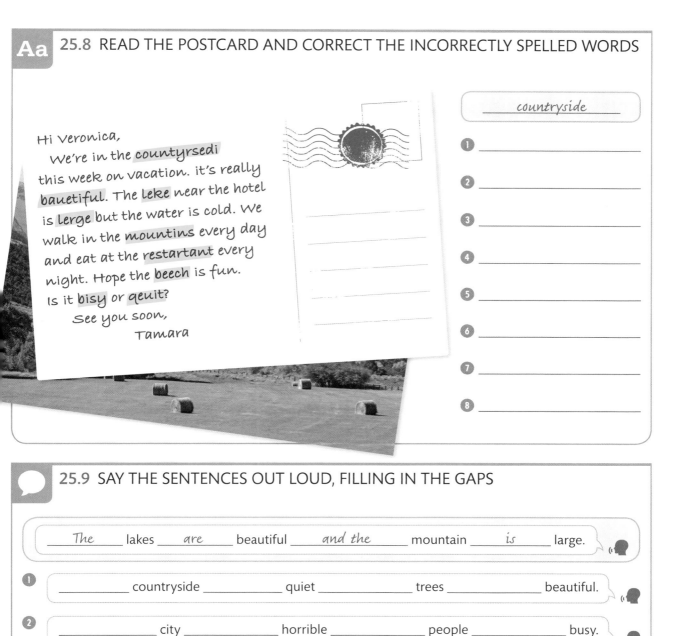

Aa 25.8 READ THE POSTCARD AND CORRECT THE INCORRECTLY SPELLED WORDS

Hi Veronica,
We're in the **countyrsedi** this week on vacation. it's really **bauetiful**. The **leke** near the hotel is **lerge** but the water is cold. We walk in the **mountins** every day and eat at the **restartant** every night. Hope the **beech** is fun. Is it **bisy** or **qeuit**?
See you soon,
Tamara

countryside

1 _____

2 _____

3 _____

4 _____

5 _____

6 _____

7 _____

8 _____

25.9 SAY THE SENTENCES OUT LOUD, FILLING IN THE GAPS

____The____ lakes ____are____ beautiful ____and the____ mountain ____is____ large.

1 _____ countryside _____ quiet _____ trees _____ beautiful.

2 _____ city _____ horrible _____ people _____ busy.

3 _____ hotel _____ new _____ swimming pool _____ large.

4 _____ beach _____ big _____ cafés _____ busy.

5 _____ city _____ old _____ buildings _____ beautiful.

95

25.10 KEY LANGUAGE USING QUANTITY PHRASES

English has many different phrases for quantities when the exact number is not known.

Use "some" when there is more than one, but you don't know exactly how many.

There are some buildings.

Use "a few" for a small number.

There are a few buildings.

Use "lots of" for a large number.

There are lots of buildings.

🔊

25.11 FURTHER EXAMPLES USING QUANTITY PHRASES

 There are some trees.

 There are lots of mountains.

 There are lots of people.

 There are a few cars.

🔊

25.12 LISTEN TO THE AUDIO, THEN NUMBER THE PICTURES IN THE ORDER THEY ARE DESCRIBED

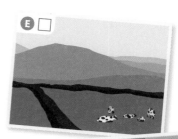

25.13 WRITE SENTENCES ABOUT THE IMAGE USING "A FEW," "SOME," OR "LOTS OF"

There are some trees.

1 _____ people.

2 _____ buildings.

3 _____ cars.

4 _____ parks.

25.14 LOOK AT THE TABLE, THEN SAY SENTENCES OUT LOUD USING "A FEW," "SOME," AND "LOTS OF"

	A FEW	SOME	LOTS OF
In Greenpoint,	🏠		🚶
1 In the tree,	🐦	🍎	
2 In the sea,	🚶		🐟
3 In the countryside,		🚶	🌳

In Greenpoint, there are a few buildings and lots of people.

26 Giving reasons

Use the conjunction "because" to give a reason for something. You can also use "because" to answer the question "Why?"

⚙ **Key language** "Because"
Aa Vocabulary Places and jobs
New skill Giving reasons

26.1 KEY LANGUAGE USING "BECAUSE"

This is the main clause.

Use "because" before you give the reason.

This is the reason.

I live in the countryside because it's beautiful.

26.2 FURTHER EXAMPLES

It's a noisy town because there are lots of cars.

My village is quiet because there are only a few families here.

The nurse is busy because there are lots of patients.

26.3 LISTEN TO THE AUDIO AND ANSWER THE QUESTIONS

Ben goes to the restaurant because...
it is near home. ☐ his friend is the chef. ☑

1 Jacob lives in Newport because his family...
lives there. ☐ lives far away. ☐

2 Marina works outside because...
she's a farmer. ☐ she's a gardener. ☐

3 Lin gets up at 6am because she...
goes running. ☐ goes swimming. ☐

4 Ho uses his laptop because...
it's new. ☐ it's old. ☐

5 Pablo is a doctor because he is good...
with people. ☐ with children. ☐

6 Annie goes to Boston because...
her aunt lives there. ☐ she's a chef. ☐

7 The countryside is quiet because there aren't...
lots of people. ☐ lots of animals. ☐

26.4 FILL IN THE GAPS USING THE PHRASES IN THE PANEL

I work in a theater because _____ *I'm an actor* _____ .

I'm a gardener

we're teachers

I'm an actor

you're busy

she's a farmer

they're students

it's quiet

she's a receptionist

1 She lives on a farm because _____ .

2 She works in a hotel because _____ .

3 They get up late because _____ .

4 We work with children because _____ .

5 You don't eat lunch because _____ .

6 I work outside because _____ .

7 My parents go to the countryside because _____ .

🔊

---

26 ✅ CHECKLIST

⚙️ "Because" ☐   **Aa** Places and jobs ☐   🧩 Giving reasons ☐

♻ REVIEW THE ENGLISH YOU HAVE LEARNED IN UNITS 21–26

NEW LANGUAGE	SAMPLE SENTENCE	☑	UNIT
USING "THERE IS" AND "THERE ARE"	There is **a hospital.** There are **three hospitals.** There isn't **a school.** There aren't any **schools.**	☐	21.1, 21.6
ARTICLES	**I work in** a library. **I work in** the library **on Main Street.**	☐	22.1
USING "ANY" AND "SOME"	**Are there** any **hotels? There are** some **hotels.**	☐	22.8
IMPERATIVES	Stop! Be **careful!**	☐	23.1
JOINING SENTENCES	**There's a library** and **a restaurant.** **There's a hotel,** but **there isn't a store.**	☐	24.1, 24.7
USING ADJECTIVES	**She is a** busy **woman. It is a** busy **town.** **The town is** busy. **It is** busy.	☐	25.1, 25.4
USING "BECAUSE"	**I live in the countryside** because **it's beautiful.**	☐	26.1

27.1 AROUND THE HOUSE

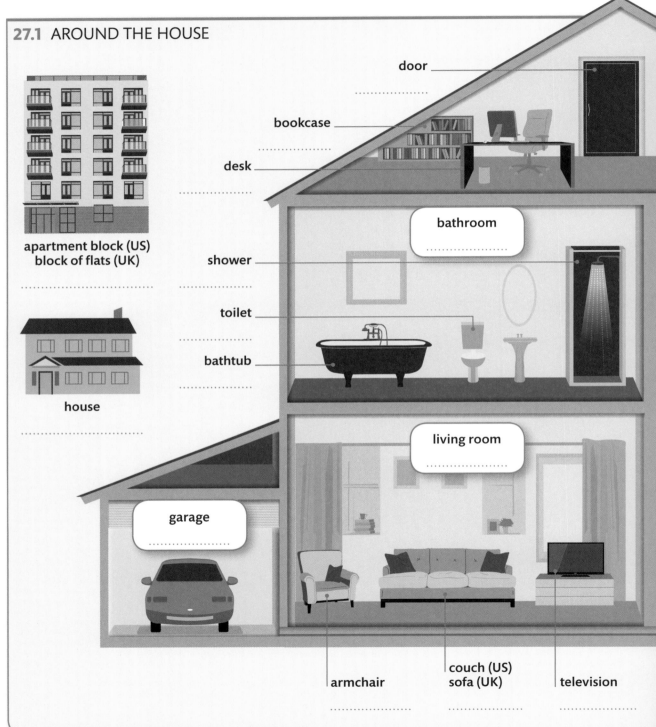

apartment block (US)
block of flats (UK)

house

door

bookcase

desk

shower

toilet

bathtub

bathroom

living room

garage

armchair

couch (US)
sofa (UK)

television

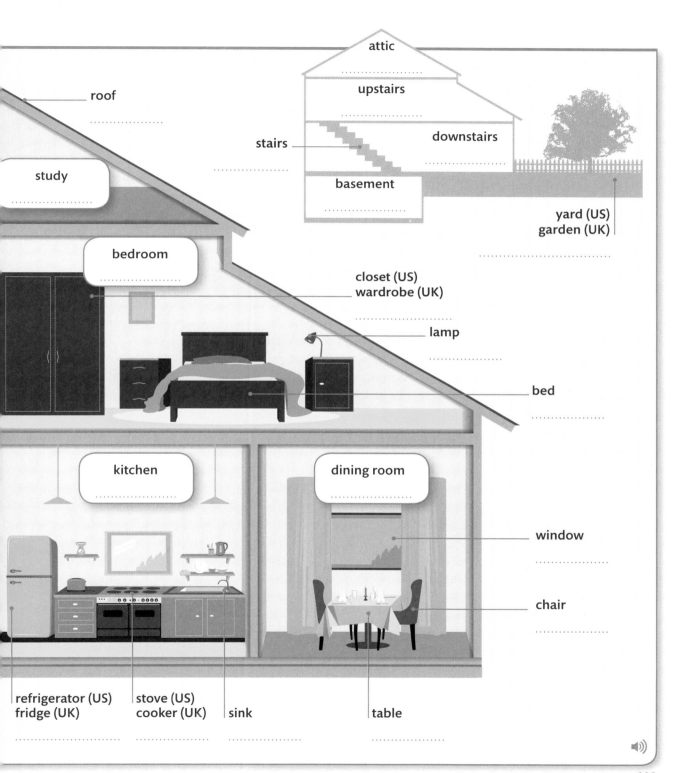

attic

roof

upstairs

study

stairs

downstairs

basement

bedroom

yard (US)
garden (UK)

closet (US)
wardrobe (UK)

lamp

bed

kitchen

dining room

window

chair

refrigerator (US)
fridge (UK)

stove (US)
cooker (UK)

sink

table

101

28 The things I have

When you talk about things you own, such as furniture or pets, you can use the verb "have." You can also use it to talk about your qualifications and the appliances and rooms in your home.

⚙ **New language** Using "have"
Aa Vocabulary Household objects
🧩 **New skill** Talking about possessions

28.1 KEY LANGUAGE USING "HAVE"

"Have" is an irregular verb. The third person singular form is "has," not "haves."

Use "has" for the third person singular (he, she, or it).

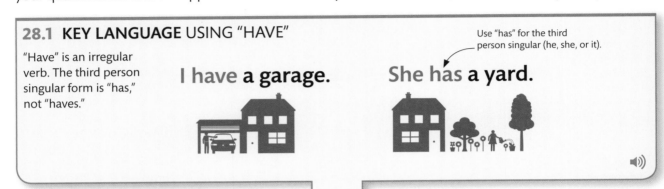

I have **a garage.**

She has **a yard.**

28.2 HOW TO FORM STATEMENTS USING "HAVE"

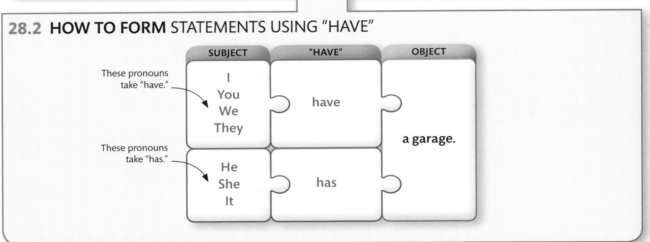

SUBJECT	"HAVE"	OBJECT
These pronouns take "have." → I You We They	have	a garage.
These pronouns take "has." → He She It	has	

28.3 FILL IN THE GAPS USING "HAVE" OR "HAS"

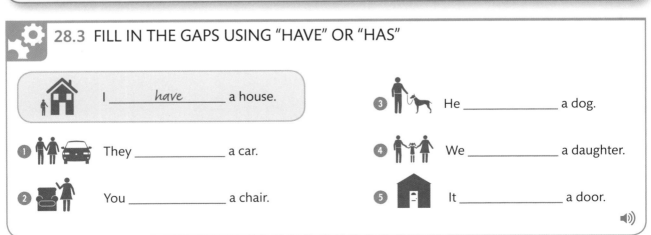

I _____*have*_____ a house.

1 They _____ a car.

2 You _____ a chair.

3 He _____ a dog.

4 We _____ a daughter.

5 It _____ a door.

Maya ✓ Ben ☐

① Maya ☐ Ben ☐

② Maya ☐ Ben ☐

③ Maya ☐ Ben ☐

④ Maya ☐ Ben ☐

28.5 READ THE ADVERTISEMENTS AND ANSWER THE QUESTIONS

Riverside Apartment has four bedrooms.
True ☐ **False** ✓

① Riverside Apartment has one bathroom.
True ☐ **False** ☐

② Lake View has a yard.
True ☐ **False** ☐

③ Lake View has a garage.
True ☐ **False** ☐

④ Stone Hill has five bedrooms.
True ☐ **False** ☐

⑤ Stone Hill has a shower.
True ☐ **False** ☐

⑥ Stone Hill has a kitchen.
True ☐ **False** ☐

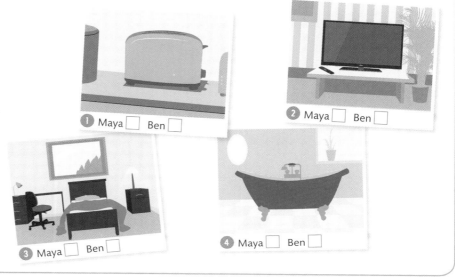

34 ACCOMMODATION

PROPERTIES TO RENT

Riverside Apartment **$800/month**
This old apartment is on the first floor of Riverside House. It has three bedrooms and two bathrooms. There's a beautiful park next door.

Lake View **$900/month**
This house is on a quiet street next to a lake. It has two bedrooms and a big kitchen in the basement. It also has a beautiful yard, but there is no garage.

Stone Hill **$1,500/month**
This house is in the old part of Bridgewater. It has four bedrooms and a bathroom with a bathtub and a shower. It also has a big kitchen. All the furniture is new and stylish.

28.6 KEY LANGUAGE "HAVE" NEGATIVES

Although "have" is irregular, its negative is formed in the usual way.
The negative form can also be contracted as with other verbs.

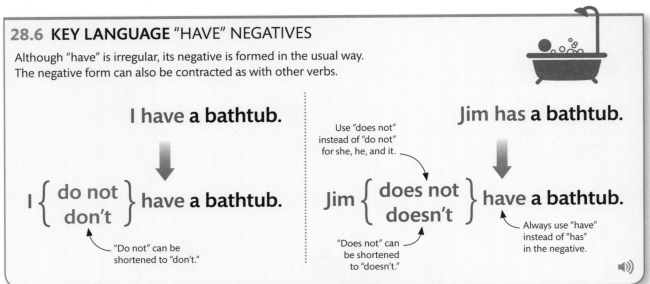

I have a bathtub.

I { do not / don't } have a bathtub.

"Do not" can be shortened to "don't."

Jim has a bathtub.

Use "does not" instead of "do not" for she, he, and it.

Jim { does not / doesn't } have a bathtub.

"Does not" can be shortened to "doesn't."

Always use "have" instead of "has" in the negative.

28.7 WRITE EACH SENTENCE IN ITS OTHER NEGATIVE FORM

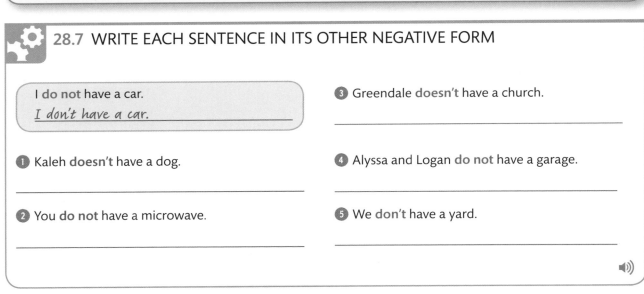

I **do not** have a car.
I don't have a car.

❶ Kaleh **doesn't** have a dog.

_____

❷ You **do not** have a microwave.

_____

❸ Greendale **doesn't** have a church.

_____

❹ Alyssa and Logan **do not** have a garage.

_____

❺ We **don't** have a yard.

_____

28.8 USE THE CHART TO CREATE 11 CORRECT SENTENCES AND SAY THEM OUT LOUD

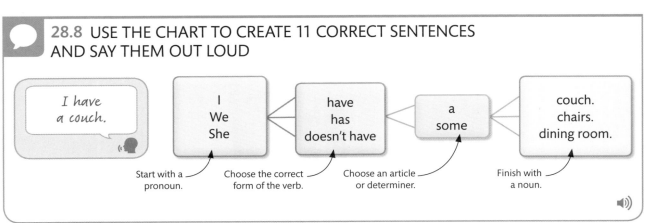

I have a couch.

| I / We / She | have / has / doesn't have | a / some | couch. / chairs. / dining room. |

Start with a pronoun.

Choose the correct form of the verb.

Choose an article or determiner.

Finish with a noun.

104

28.9 ANOTHER WAY TO SAY "HAVE"

Some English speakers, especially in the UK, use "have got" instead of "have." It means the same thing.

We $\left\{ \begin{array}{l} \text{have} \\ \text{have got} \end{array} \right\}$ a dog.

The only difference is the word "got."

28.10 HOW TO FORM "HAVE GOT"

POSITIVE	NEGATIVE
I have got **a dog.**	He has not got **a dog.**
I've got **a dog.**	He hasn't got **a dog.**

Only use this form when using "have" with "got." Don't shorten "I have" to "I've a dog."

"Has not got" can be shortened to "hasn't got."

28.11 WRITE EACH SENTENCE IN ITS OTHER TWO FORMS

She **has** a computer.	She has got a computer.	She's got a computer.
① They **don't have** a couch.		
② He **has** three sisters.		
③ You **don't have** a bike.		
④ We **have** a microwave.		
⑤ It **has** a bathtub.		
⑥ They **have** a cat.		

28 ✓ CHECKLIST

✿ Using "have" ☐   **Aa** Household objects ☐   ✦ Talking about possessions ☐

What do you have?

Use questions with "have" to ask someone about the things they own. "Do" or "does" are used to form the question.

⚙ **New language** "Have" questions
Aa Vocabulary House and furniture
🧩 **New skill** Asking about household objects

29.1 KEY LANGUAGE ASKING "HAVE" QUESTIONS

Form "have" questions by adding "do" or "does."

"Has" changes to "have" in questions.

You have a TV.

⬇

Do you have a TV?

Add "do" to turn "I," "you," "we," and "they" statements into questions.

She has a TV.

⬇

Does she have a TV?

Add "does" to form questions for "he," "she," and "it."

29.2 VOCABULARY HOUSEHOLD OBJECTS

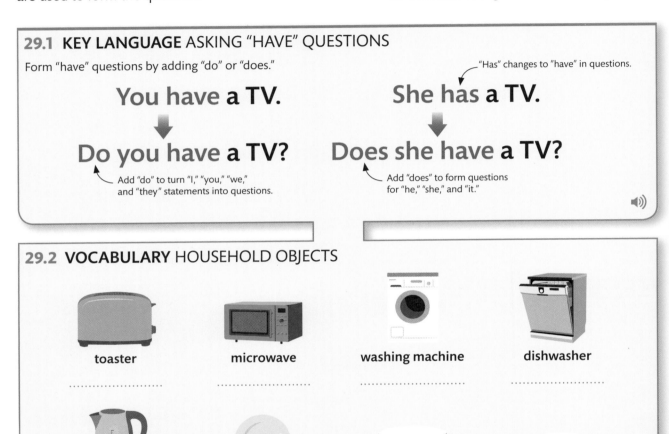

toaster

microwave

washing machine

dishwasher

kettle

plate

bowl

cup

silverware (US)
cutlery (UK)

knife

fork

spoon

29.3 REWRITE THE SENTENCES AS QUESTIONS

She has an oven.
Does she have an oven?

1 They have a toaster.
_____

2 You have a new couch.
_____

3 Ben has a washing machine.
_____

4 We have an old armchair.
_____

5 Karen has a large TV.
_____

6 The kitchen has a sink.
_____

7 The house has a yard.
_____

◀))

29.4 LISTEN AND MARK WHO OWNS WHICH OBJECTS

Tim ✓   Lucy ☐

3 Tim ☐   Lucy ☐

1 Tim ☐   Lucy ☐

4 Tim ☐   Lucy ☐

2 Tim ☐   Lucy ☐

5 Tim ☐   Lucy ☐

29.5 USE THE CHART TO CREATE NINE CORRECT SENTENCES AND SAY THEM OUT LOUD

Do you have any chairs? «👤

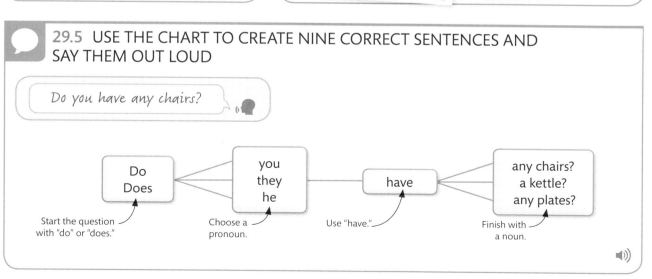

| Do / Does | you / they / he | have | any chairs? / a kettle? / any plates? |

Start the question with "do" or "does."

Choose a pronoun.

Use "have."

Finish with a noun.

◀))

107

29.6 KEY LANGUAGE SHORT ANSWERS TO "HAVE" QUESTIONS

You can give short answers to "have" questions using "do" and "don't."

Add "do" to form a question.

Do you have a microwave?

Use "do" in the positive answer.

Yes, I do.

No, I don't.

Use "do not" or "don't" in the negative answer.

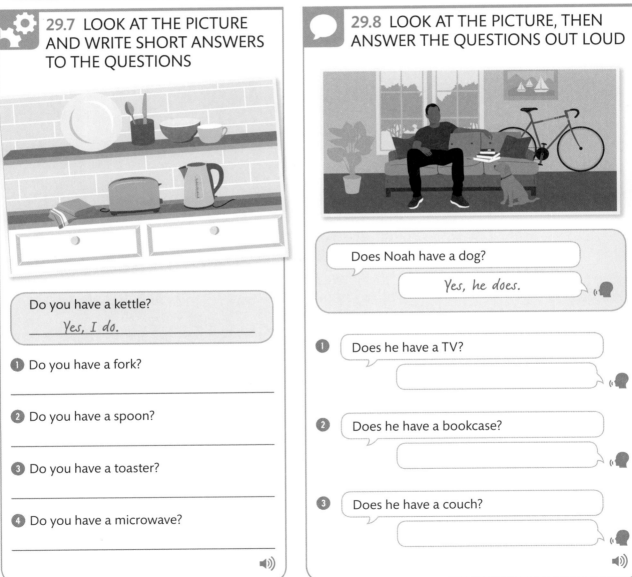

29.7 LOOK AT THE PICTURE AND WRITE SHORT ANSWERS TO THE QUESTIONS

Do you have a kettle?

Yes, I do.

1 Do you have a fork?

_____

2 Do you have a spoon?

_____

3 Do you have a toaster?

_____

4 Do you have a microwave?

_____

29.8 LOOK AT THE PICTURE, THEN ANSWER THE QUESTIONS OUT LOUD

Does Noah have a dog?

Yes, he does.

1 Does he have a TV?

2 Does he have a bookcase?

3 Does he have a couch?

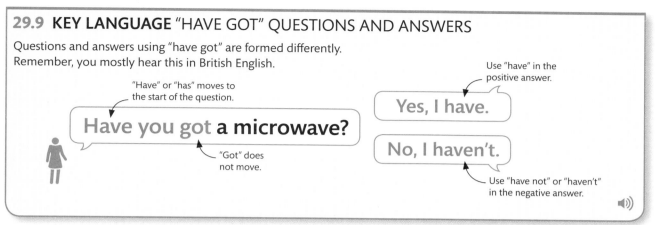

29.9 KEY LANGUAGE "HAVE GOT" QUESTIONS AND ANSWERS

Questions and answers using "have got" are formed differently.
Remember, you mostly hear this in British English.

"Have" or "has" moves to the start of the question.

Have you got a microwave?

"Got" does not move.

Use "have" in the positive answer.

Yes, I have.

No, I haven't.

Use "have not" or "haven't" in the negative answer.

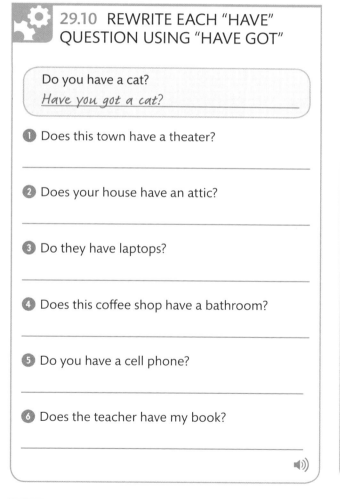

29.10 REWRITE EACH "HAVE" QUESTION USING "HAVE GOT"

Do you have a cat?
Have you got a cat?

① Does this town have a theater?

_____

② Does your house have an attic?

_____

③ Do they have laptops?

_____

④ Does this coffee shop have a bathroom?

_____

⑤ Do you have a cell phone?

_____

⑥ Does the teacher have my book?

_____

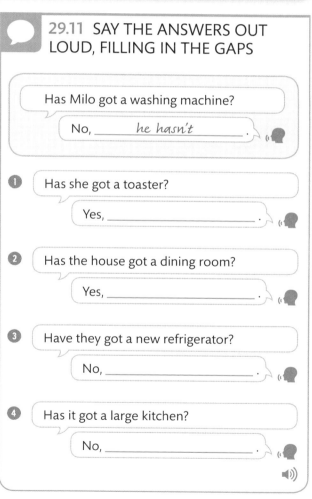

29.11 SAY THE ANSWERS OUT LOUD, FILLING IN THE GAPS

Has Milo got a washing machine?

No, _____ _he hasn't_ _____ .

① Has she got a toaster?

Yes, _____ .

② Has the house got a dining room?

Yes, _____ .

③ Have they got a new refrigerator?

No, _____ .

④ Has it got a large kitchen?

No, _____ .

---

29 ✓ CHECKLIST

⚙ "Have" questions ☐   **Aa** House and furniture ☐   🧩 Asking about household objects ☐

30 Vocabulary

30.1 FOOD AND DRINK

food

drinks

breakfast

lunch

dinner

meat

fish

seafood

fruit

vegetables

bread

pasta

rice

noodles

potatoes

milk

cheese

butter

yogurt

eggs

sugar

cookie (US)
biscuit (UK)

chocolate

cake

cereal

orange

apple

banana

strawberry

mango

sandwich

burger

fries (US)
chips (UK)

spaghetti

salad

coffee

tea

juice

water

lemonade

31 Counting

In English, nouns can be countable or uncountable. Countable nouns can be individually counted. Objects that can't be separated and counted are uncountable.

⚙ **New language** Uncountable nouns
Aa **Vocabulary** Food containers
🧩 **New skill** Talking about food

31.1 KEY LANGUAGE COUNTABLE AND UNCOUNTABLE NOUNS

Use "a," "an," or a number to talk about countable nouns.
"Some" can be used for both countable and uncountable nouns.

COUNTABLE NOUNS

There is an egg.

There are four eggs.

There are some eggs.

Use "some" when there are more countable things than you can easily count.

UNCOUNTABLE NOUNS

Uncountable nouns are always paired with verbs in the singular.

There is some rice.

Always use "some" with uncountable nouns, not "a," "an," or a number.

31.2 FURTHER EXAMPLES COUNTABLE AND UNCOUNTABLE NOUNS

 a sandwich   an apple

 four bananas   two burgers

 some milk   some water

 some spaghetti   some sugar

⚙ 31.3 CROSS OUT THE INCORRECT WORD IN EACH SENTENCE

Michael has ~~two~~ / some milk.

❶ Jake has an / some apple.

❷ There is a / some coffee.

❸ Reena eats a / some spaghetti.

❹ There are two / some eggs.

❺ I've got a / some bananas.

31.4 KEY LANGUAGE NEGATIVES AND QUESTIONS

For both countable and uncountable nouns, use "any" in negative sentences and questions.

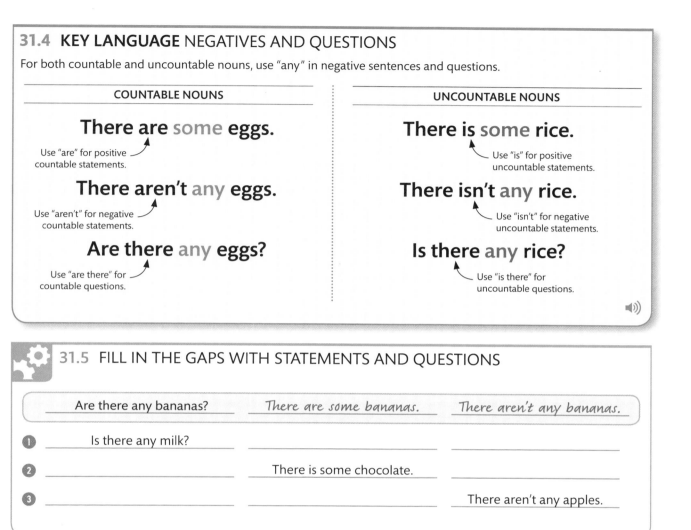

COUNTABLE NOUNS

There are some eggs.

Use "are" for positive countable statements.

There aren't any eggs.

Use "aren't" for negative countable statements.

Are there any eggs?

Use "are there" for countable questions.

UNCOUNTABLE NOUNS

There is some rice.

Use "is" for positive uncountable statements.

There isn't any rice.

Use "isn't" for negative uncountable statements.

Is there any rice?

Use "is there" for uncountable questions.

31.5 FILL IN THE GAPS WITH STATEMENTS AND QUESTIONS

Are there any bananas?	There are some bananas.	There aren't any bananas.
1 Is there any milk?		
2	There is some chocolate.	
3		There aren't any apples.

31.6 ANSWER THE QUESTIONS BY FILLING IN THE GAPS, SPEAKING OUT LOUD

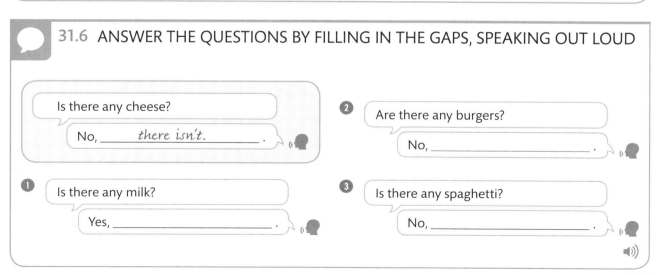

Is there any cheese?

No, _____*there isn't.*_____ .

2 Are there any burgers?

No, _____ .

1 Is there any milk?

Yes, _____ .

3 Is there any spaghetti?

No, _____ .

31.7 VOCABULARY FOOD CONTAINERS

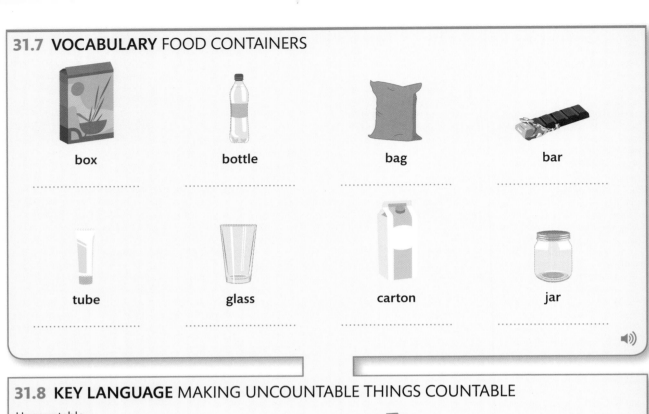

box

bottle

bag

bar

tube

glass

carton

jar

31.8 KEY LANGUAGE MAKING UNCOUNTABLE THINGS COUNTABLE

Uncountable nouns can be made countable if they are placed in containers.

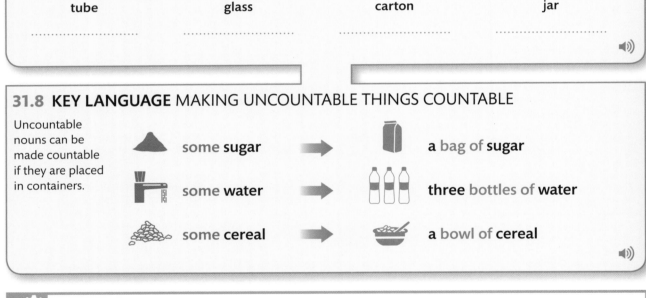

some **sugar** ➡ a bag of **sugar**

some **water** ➡ three bottles of **water**

some **cereal** ➡ a bowl of **cereal**

31.9 FILL IN THE GAPS TO COMPLETE THE SENTENCES

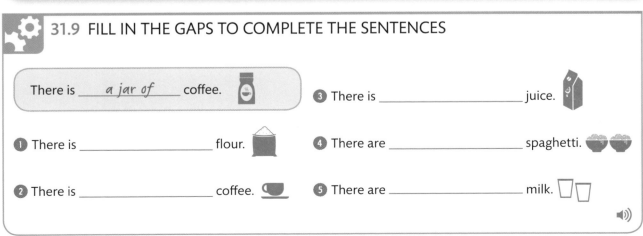

There is ____a jar of____ coffee.

❶ There is _____ flour.

❷ There is _____ coffee.

❸ There is _____ juice.

❹ There are _____ spaghetti.

❺ There are _____ milk.

31.10 KEY LANGUAGE QUESTIONS ABOUT QUANTITIES

You use "many" to ask questions about quantities of countable nouns,
and "much" to ask questions about quantities of uncountable nouns.

How many eggs are there?

Use "many" for countable questions.

How much rice is there?

Use "much" for uncountable questions.

🔊

31.11 FURTHER EXAMPLES QUESTIONS ABOUT QUANTITIES

How many cupcakes are there?

How much pasta is there?

How many apples are there?

How much chocolate is there?

🔊

31.12 FILL IN THE GAPS USING "HOW MUCH" AND "HOW MANY"

How much _____ pizza is there?

1 _____ glasses of juice are there?

2 _____ water is there?

3 _____ potatoes are there?

4 _____ bars of chocolate are there?

5 _____ pasta is there?

6 _____ cartons of juice are there?

7 _____ milk is there?

🔊

31.13 LISTEN TO THE AUDIO AND ANSWER THE QUESTIONS

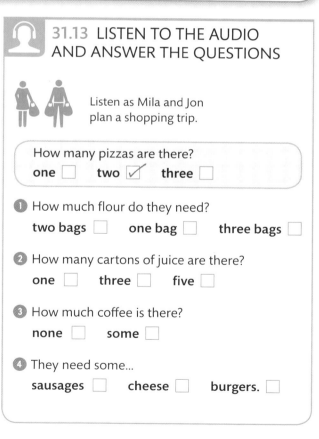

Listen as Mila and Jon plan a shopping trip.

How many pizzas are there?
one ☐   two ☑   three ☐

1 How much flour do they need?
two bags ☐   one bag ☐   three bags ☐

2 How many cartons of juice are there?
one ☐   three ☐   five ☐

3 How much coffee is there?
none ☐   some ☐

4 They need some…
sausages ☐   cheese ☐   burgers. ☐

31 ✓ CHECKLIST

⚙ Uncountable nouns ☐   **Aa** Food containers ☐   🧩 Talking about food ☐

32 Measuring

Use "enough" when you have the correct number or amount of something. Use "too many" or "too much" if you have more than enough.

⚙ **New language** Measurements
Aa Vocabulary Ingredients and quantities
🧩 **New skill** Talking about amounts

32.1 KEY LANGUAGE "ENOUGH / TOO MANY"

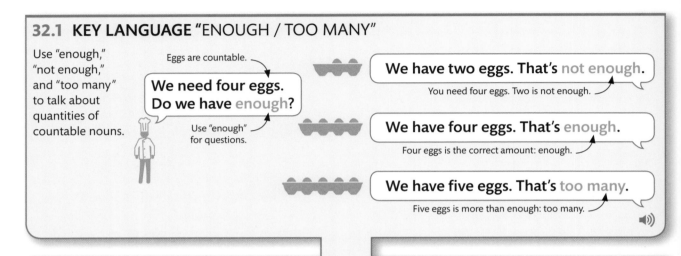

Use "enough," "not enough," and "too many" to talk about quantities of countable nouns.

Eggs are countable.

We need four eggs. Do we have enough?

Use "enough" for questions.

We have two eggs. That's not enough.
You need four eggs. Two is not enough.

We have four eggs. That's enough.
Four eggs is the correct amount: enough.

We have five eggs. That's too many.
Five eggs is more than enough: too many.

🔊

32.2 FURTHER EXAMPLES "ENOUGH / TOO MANY"

There are enough eggs.

You have enough eggs.

There aren't enough eggs.

You don't have enough eggs.

There are too many eggs.

You have too many eggs.

🔊

32.3 READ THE RECIPE AND CROSS OUT THE INCORRECT WORDS IN EACH SENTENCE

There ~~aren't enough~~ / are too many mangoes.

① There aren't enough / are enough oranges.

② You have enough / too many pineapples.

③ There aren't enough / are too many apples.

④ You don't have enough / too many bananas.

FRUIT SALAD RECIPE
2 apples
4 oranges
1 pineapple
3 bananas
1 mango

🔊

32.4 KEY LANGUAGE "ENOUGH / TOO MUCH"

Use "enough," "not enough," and "too much" to talk about quantities of uncountable nouns.

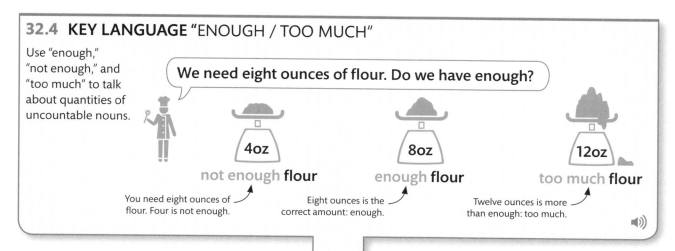

We need eight ounces of flour. Do we have enough?

4oz not enough **flour**

You need eight ounces of flour. Four is not enough.

8oz enough **flour**

Eight ounces is the correct amount: enough.

12oz too much **flour**

Twelve ounces is more than enough: too much.

32.5 FURTHER EXAMPLES "ENOUGH / TOO MUCH"

There is enough **flour.**

They have enough **flour.**

There isn't enough **flour.**

They don't **have** enough **flour.**

There is too much **flour.**

They have too much **flour.**

32.6 LISTEN AND MATCH THE PICTURES TO THE AMOUNTS

Sheila and Vikram are preparing to bake a cake.

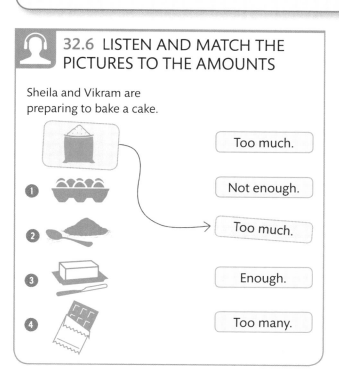

Too much.

Not enough.

Too much.

Enough.

Too many.

32.7 CROSS OUT THE INCORRECT WORDS IN EACH SENTENCE

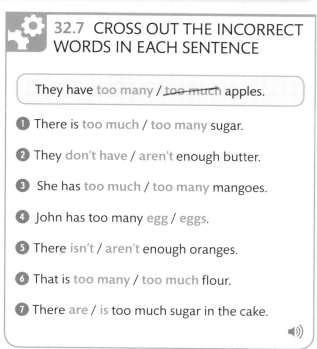

They have too many / ~~too much~~ apples.

❶ There is too much / too many sugar.

❷ They don't have / aren't enough butter.

❸ She has too much / too many mangoes.

❹ John has too many egg / eggs.

❺ There isn't / aren't enough oranges.

❻ That is too many / too much flour.

❼ There are / is too much sugar in the cake.

33.1 CLOTHES AND ACCESSORIES

t-shirt

blouse

shirt

dress

skirt

pants (US)
trousers (UK)

jeans

jacket

coat

raincoat

socks

boots

shoes

sandals

sneakers (US)
trainers (UK)

scarf

hat

gloves

belt

purse (US)
handbag (UK)

33.2 CLOTHING SIZES

extra small
....

small
....

medium
....

large
....

extra large
....

33.3 DESCRIBING CLOTHES

smart
....

casual
....

suit
....

uniform
....

short sleeves
....

long sleeves
....

cheap
....

expensive
....

33.4 COLORS (US) / COLOURS (UK)

red
....

orange
....

yellow
....

green
....

blue
....

purple
....

pink
....

white
....

gray (US)
grey (UK)
....

black
....

34 At the shops

You can use many different verbs to talk about what happens when you are shopping. Use "too" and "enough" to describe how well clothes fit you.

✿ **New language** Using "too" and "fit"
Aa Vocabulary Shopping and clothes
New skill Describing clothes

34.1 VOCABULARY SHOPPING VERBS

Ana owns a red hat.

Choose a new shirt!

Luc sells old clothes.

They want new shoes.

The hat fits Jane.

Let's buy some hats!

34.2 CROSS OUT THE INCORRECT WORD IN EACH SENTENCE

Tsuru ~~want~~ / wants a green jumper.

1 Hannah **choose** / **chooses** a yellow skirt.

2 Elliot and Ruby **buy** / **buys** a new couch.

3 Sue **own** / **owns** an old winter coat.

4 Jess's dad **buy** / **buys** her a new bike.

5 Chris and Lisa **own** / **owns** a black sports car.

6 Gayle and Mike **sell** / **sells** shoes at the market.

7 Mia **choose** / **chooses** her red shoes.

8 The shoes **fit** / **fits** me.

9 We **want** / **wants** new white shirts.

34.3 REWRITE THE SENTENCES, PUTTING THE WORDS IN THE CORRECT ORDER

She | a | green | long | dress | buys

She buys a long green dress.

1 They | expensive | sweaters. | blue | choose

_____

2 some | brown | old | hats. | has | Judith

_____

3 sells | This | shop | short | red | pants.

_____

4 owns | Tina | black | cheap | shoes.

_____

5 Jim | buys | black | new | a | coat

_____

◀))

Aa 34.4 READ THE MESSAGES AND CIRCLE 12 ADJECTIVES

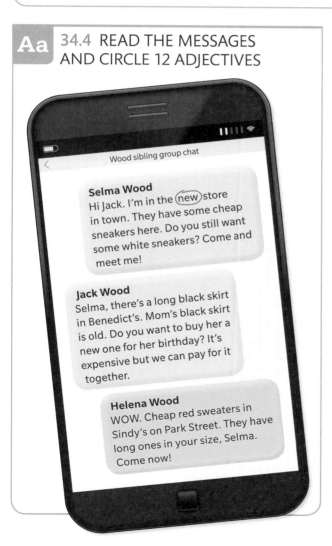

Wood sibling group chat

Selma Wood
Hi Jack. I'm in the (new) store in town. They have some cheap sneakers here. Do you still want some white sneakers? Come and meet me!

Jack Wood
Selma, there's a long black skirt in Benedict's. Mom's black skirt is old. Do you want to buy her a new one for her birthday? It's expensive but we can pay for it together.

Helena Wood
WOW. Cheap red sweaters in Sindy's on Park Street. They have long ones in your size, Selma. Come now!

34.5 LISTEN TO THE AUDIO AND ANSWER THE QUESTIONS

Five groups of friends are talking about the things they want to buy.

What type of dress does Marie buy?
short ☐
long ☑

1 Which hat do the friends choose for Shala?
a red hat ☐
a blue hat ☐

2 What does Ben want?
black shoes ☐
a new t-shirt ☐

3 What does Gemma want?
a cheap shirt ☐
a cheap skirt ☐

4 Which coat does Joe buy?
a blue coat ☐
a black coat ☐

121

34.6 KEY LANGUAGE ANSWERING "DOES IT FIT?"

In English, you use "enough" and "too" with adjectives
to describe how well a piece of clothing fits you.

The noun comes first when
asking if something is the correct size.

Does the sweater fit?

No, it is not big enough.

Is the sweater too small?

No, it is big enough.

Does the sweater fit?

No, it is too big.

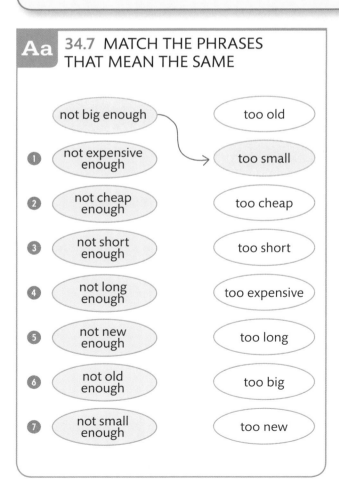

Aa 34.7 MATCH THE PHRASES THAT MEAN THE SAME

not big enough ——→ too small

too old

1 not expensive enough

2 not cheap enough — too cheap

3 not short enough — too short

4 not long enough — too expensive

5 not new enough — too long

6 not old enough — too big

7 not small enough — too new

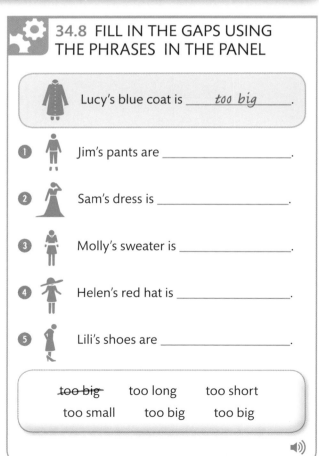

34.8 FILL IN THE GAPS USING THE PHRASES IN THE PANEL

Lucy's blue coat is ___*too big*___.

1 Jim's pants are _____.

2 Sam's dress is _____.

3 Molly's sweater is _____.

4 Helen's red hat is _____.

5 Lili's shoes are _____.

~~too big~~   too long   too short

too small   too big   too big

34.9 LISTEN TO THE AUDIO AND MARK WHICH PIECE OF CLOTHING EACH PERSON DESCRIBES

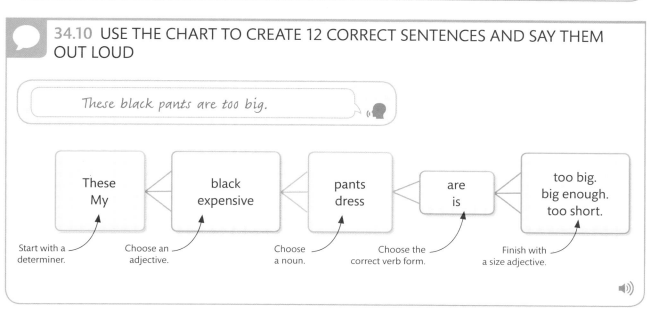

34.10 USE THE CHART TO CREATE 12 CORRECT SENTENCES AND SAY THEM OUT LOUD

These black pants are too big.

These / My	black / expensive	pants / dress	are / is	too big. / big enough. / too short.

Start with a determiner.

Choose an adjective.

Choose a noun.

Choose the correct verb form.

Finish with a size adjective.

34 ✔ CHECKLIST

⚙ Using "too" and "fit" ☐   **Aa** Shopping and clothes ☐   🧩 Describing clothes ☐

35 Describing things

You can use adjectives to give your opinion about things as well as to give factual information. You can use more than one adjective before a noun.

⚙ New language Opinion adjectives
Aa Vocabulary Shopping and materials
🧩 New skill Giving opinions

35.1 KEY LANGUAGE OPINION ADJECTIVES

Some adjectives give opinions, not facts.

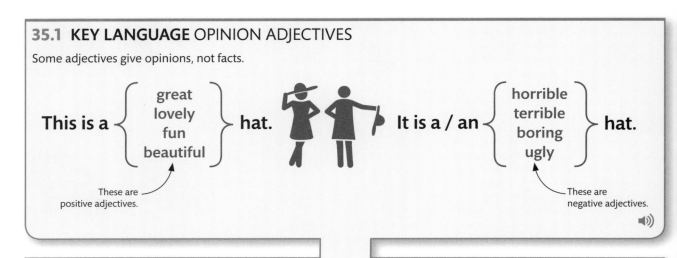

This is a { great / lovely / fun / beautiful } **hat.**

These are positive adjectives.

It is a / an { horrible / terrible / boring / ugly } **hat.**

These are negative adjectives.

35.2 KEY LANGUAGE ADJECTIVE ORDER

Adjectives usually follow a set order in English.
Opinion adjectives come before fact adjectives.

	OPINION ADJECTIVE	FACT ADJECTIVE	NOUN
This is a	**lovely**	**green**	**hat.**

Opinion adjectives come first.

Fact adjectives come last.

35.3 FURTHER EXAMPLES ADJECTIVE ORDER

 It is a lovely big house.

 We have a horrible old car.

 This is a great new book.

 Natalie has a beautiful old cat.

 They are ugly purple shoes.

 He is a brilliant young actor.

35.4 CROSS OUT THE INCORRECT ADJECTIVE IN EACH SENTENCE

It is a good / ~~bad~~ young dog.

❸ I have a lovely / horrible long dress.

❶ This is a lovely / horrible old t-shirt.

❹ This is a beautiful / ugly bird.

❷ This is a boring / great movie.

❺ This is a fun / boring party.

35.5 REWRITE THE SENTENCES, PUTTING THE WORDS IN THE CORRECT ORDER

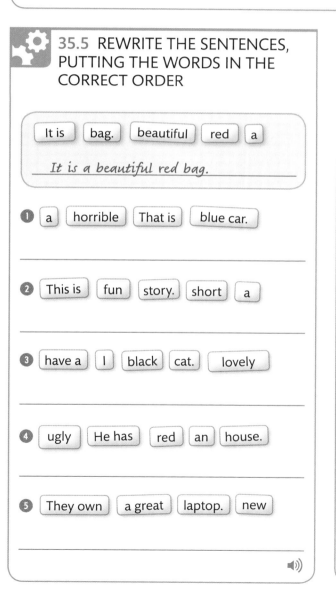

| It is | bag. | beautiful | red | a |

It is a beautiful red bag.

❶ | a | horrible | That is | blue car. |

_____

❷ | This is | fun | story. | short | a |

_____

❸ | have a | I | black | cat. | lovely |

_____

❹ | ugly | He has | red | an | house. |

_____

❺ | They own | a great | laptop. | new |

_____

35.6 LISTEN TO THE AUDIO AND MARK THE CORRECT ANSWERS

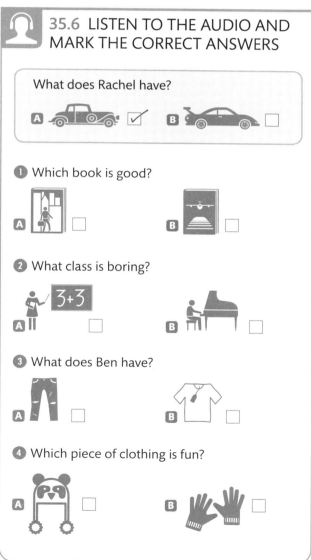

What does Rachel have?

A ✓   B ☐

❶ Which book is good?

A ☐   B ☐

❷ What class is boring?

3+3

A ☐   B ☐

❸ What does Ben have?

A ☐   B ☐

❹ Which piece of clothing is fun?

A ☐   B ☐

35.7 VOCABULARY MATERIALS

Some words can be used both as nouns to name materials, and as adjectives to say what things are made of. Two of the nouns below change when they become adjectives: "wood" to "wooden", and "wool" to "woolen".

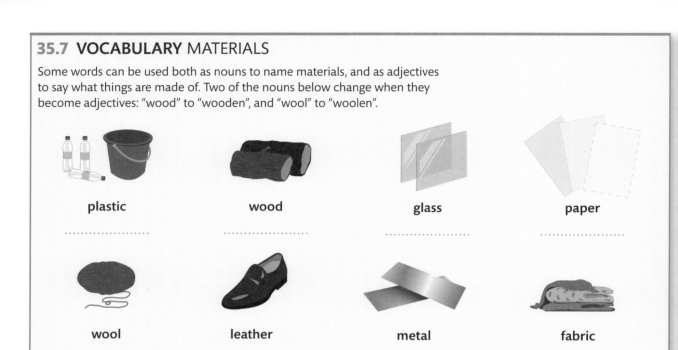

plastic

wood

glass

paper

wool

leather

metal

fabric

Aa 35.8 MATCH THE PICTURES TO THE CORRECT DESCRIPTIONS

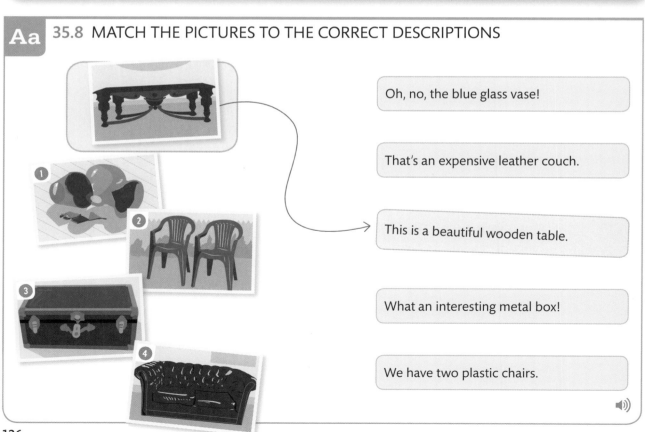

Oh, no, the blue glass vase!

That's an expensive leather couch.

This is a beautiful wooden table.

What an interesting metal box!

We have two plastic chairs.

35.9 SAY THE SENTENCES OUT LOUD, CORRECTING THE WORD ORDER

We have lovely two purple couches.

We have two lovely purple couches.

❶ She owns some wooden beautiful chairs.

❷ We own don't those plastic plates horrible.

❸ They have yellow an ugly car.

❹ He wears a blue boring sweater.

❺ She wants a metal lamp new.

❻ He owns a fabric large bag.

❼ Norah new a leather wants jacket.

---

35 ✓ CHECKLIST

⚙️ Opinion adjectives ☐   **Aa** Shopping and materials ☐   🧩 Giving opinions ☐

🔁 REVIEW THE ENGLISH YOU HAVE LEARNED IN UNITS 28–35

NEW LANGUAGE	SAMPLE SENTENCE	☑	UNIT
USING "HAVE"	I have **a garage.** She has **a yard.** I do not **have a bathtub.**	☐	28.1, 28.6
ASKING "HAVE" QUESTIONS	Do you have a TV?	☐	29.1
COUNTABLE AND UNCOUNTABLE NOUNS	There are four **eggs.** There is some **rice.** Are there any **eggs?** Is there any **rice?**	☐	31.1, 31.4
USING "ENOUGH" AND "MANY"	We have enough **eggs.** We have too many **eggs.**	☐	32.1
SHOPPING VERBS	Ana owns **a red hat.** Luc sells **old clothes.** They want **new shoes.** The hat fits **Jane.**	☐	34.1
ADJECTIVE ORDER	This is a lovely green **hat.**	☐	35.1

36.1 SPORTS

swimming

sailing

skateboarding

running

skiing

snowboarding

roller-skating

surfing

tennis

golf

badminton

baseball

basketball

soccer (US)
football (UK)

football (US)
American
football (UK)

rugby

volleyball

cycling

ice hockey

horse riding

36.2 EQUIPMENT

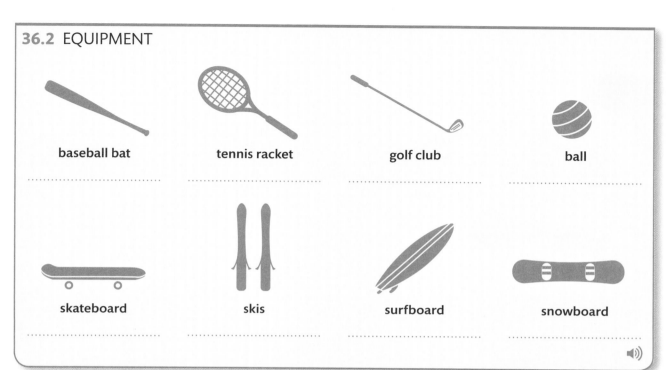

baseball bat

tennis racket

golf club

ball

skateboard

skis

surfboard

snowboard

36.3 VENUES

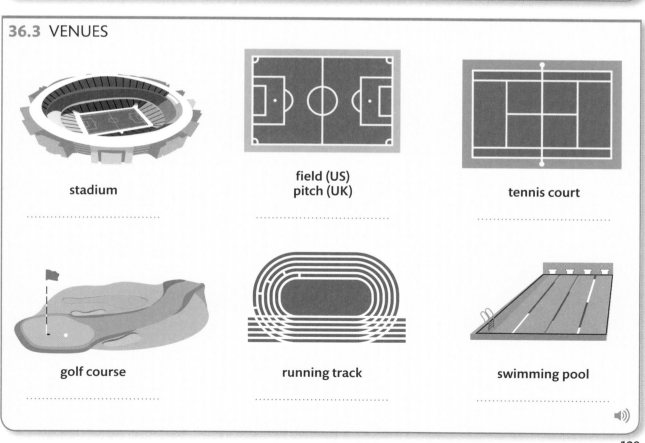

stadium

field (US)
pitch (UK)

tennis court

golf course

running track

swimming pool

37 Talking about sports

To describe taking part in some sports, you use the verb "go" plus the gerund. For other sports, you use "play" plus the noun.

⚙ **New language** "Go" and "play"
Aa Vocabulary Sports
🧩 **New skill** Talking about sports

37.1 KEY LANGUAGE "GO" WITH A GERUND

You can make some verbs into nouns by adding "-ing" to their base forms. These are called gerunds.

"Go" changes with the subject.

She goes surfing on the weekend.

Add "-ing" to the base form of the verb.

37.2 FURTHER EXAMPLES "GO" WITH A GERUND

 I go swimming **once a week.**

 We don't go fishing **at the lake.**

 He goes skateboarding **twice a month.**

 He doesn't go cycling **with his brothers.**

Do they **go dancing on Saturday nights?**

 Does she go sailing **in the summer?**

37.3 FILL IN THE GAPS TO COMPLETE THE SENTENCES

Tamara _____*goes*_____ swimming in the sea.

❶ We don't _____ surfing in the winter.

❷ Do you _____ sailing on the weekend?

❸ Tipo _____ cycling five times a week.

 ❹ He _____ fishing on the river.

❺ Sharon _____ dancing with her friend.

❻ Do they _____ running every morning?

❼ He doesn't _____ horse riding.

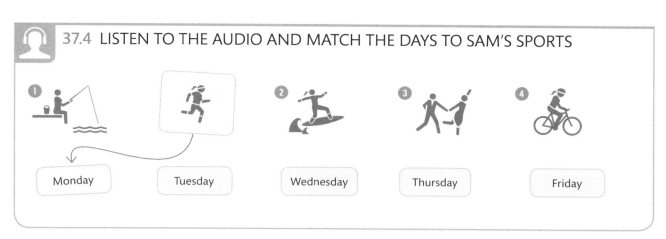

37.4 LISTEN TO THE AUDIO AND MATCH THE DAYS TO SAM'S SPORTS

Monday Tuesday Wednesday Thursday Friday

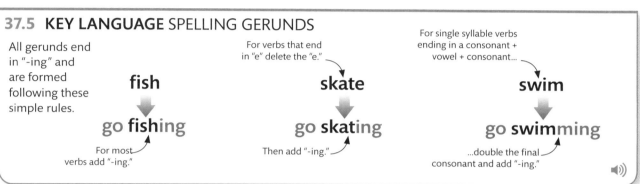

37.5 KEY LANGUAGE SPELLING GERUNDS

All gerunds end in "-ing" and are formed following these simple rules.

For verbs that end in "e" delete the "e."

For single syllable verbs ending in a consonant + vowel + consonant...

fish

skate

swim

go **fish**ing

go **skat**ing

go **swim**ming

For most verbs add "-ing."

Then add "-ing."

...double the final consonant and add "-ing."

Aa 37.6 FIND NINE HIDDEN WORDS AND WRITE THEM IN THE CORRECT GROUP

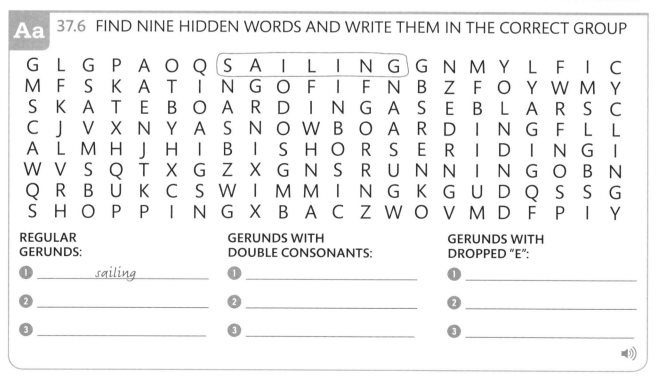

G	L	G	P	A	O	Q	S	A	I	L	I	N	G	G	N	M	Y	L	F	I	C
M	F	S	K	A	T	I	N	G	O	F	I	F	N	B	Z	F	O	Y	W	M	Y
S	K	A	T	E	B	O	A	R	D	I	N	G	A	S	E	B	L	A	R	S	C
C	J	V	X	N	Y	A	S	N	O	W	B	O	A	R	D	I	N	G	F	L	L
A	L	M	H	J	H	I	B	I	S	H	O	R	S	E	R	I	D	I	N	G	I
W	V	S	Q	T	X	G	Z	X	G	N	S	R	U	N	N	I	N	G	O	B	N
Q	R	B	U	K	C	S	W	I	M	M	I	N	G	K	G	U	D	Q	S	S	G
S	H	O	P	P	I	N	G	X	B	A	C	Z	W	O	V	M	D	F	P	I	Y

REGULAR GERUNDS:

1. _sailing_
2. _____
3. _____

GERUNDS WITH DOUBLE CONSONANTS:

1. _____
2. _____
3. _____

GERUNDS WITH DROPPED "E":

1. _____
2. _____
3. _____

37.7 KEY LANGUAGE "PLAY" WITH A NOUN

For some sports, especially ball games and competitions, you use "play" with the noun.

"Play" changes, depending on the subject.

The noun is placed after the verb.

They play tennis on Sundays.

37.8 FURTHER EXAMPLES "PLAY" WITH A NOUN

 I don't play tennis in winter.

 He plays baseball for the town.

 Does Dani play hockey on Mondays?

 Sala plays golf on Tuesday mornings.

 Do Ben and Si play chess together?

 We don't play badminton any more.

37.9 CROSS OUT THE INCORRECT WORD IN EACH SENTENCE

I ~~plays~~ / play football in the park.

1. Shala **don't** / **doesn't play** tennis.

2. Mina **plays** / **play** golf at the club.

3. We **plays** / **play** squash on Mondays.

4. The dog **plays** / **play** with its ball.

5. Maria **don't** / **doesn't play** tennis.

6. The kids **don't** / **doesn't play** games at school.

7. They **play** / **plays** soccer at the park.

37.10 REWRITE THE SENTENCES, CORRECTING THE ERRORS

He **don't play** hockey in the summer.
He doesn't play hockey in the summer.

1. We **plays** tennis every Tuesday night.

   _____

2. They **doesn't play** golf during the week.

   _____

3. You **doesn't play** volleyball at the beach.

   _____

4. Do they **plays** together every Saturday?

   _____

37.11 READ THE ARTICLE AND ANSWER THE QUESTIONS

Who plays squash on Mondays and Fridays?

James ✓   **Sara** ☐   **Chas** ☐   **Cassie** ☐

1 Who plays golf?

James ☐   **Sara** ☐   **Chas** ☐   **Cassie** ☐

2 Who goes running in the park?

James ☐   **Sara** ☐   **Chas** ☐   **Cassie** ☐

3 Who goes swimming on Thursdays?

James ☐   **Sara** ☐   **Chas** ☐   **Cassie** ☐

4 Who plays badminton?

James ☐   **Sara** ☐   **Chas** ☐   **Cassie** ☐

YOUR SPORTS

Littleton's Sports Scene

Some local residents tell us about their sports routines

I go to Belgrade Sports. It's a great place to exercise. I play squash on Mondays and Fridays.
JAMES

I love Highfields Sports. I go swimming five days a week, from Monday to Friday. I play golf on Saturdays and I play tennis on Sundays. I really like it there!
SARA

Lots of my friends go to the park and some of them play football there. I go running there. It's great.
CHAS

I like badminton and skating. I can do both at Littleton Sports. I go swimming there on Tuesdays and Fridays because there's a nice pool, and I play football on Wednesdays.
CASSIE

37.12 SAY THE SENTENCES OUT LOUD, USING "GO" OR "PLAY" AND THE CORRECT FORMS OF THE VERBS IN BRACKETS

I ___go dancing___ (dance) with my friends on Mondays.

1 Milo and I _____ (cycle) in the park on Saturdays.

2 The team _____ (football) from 6pm to 7pm on Wednesdays.

3 Imelda _____ (horse ride) once a month.

4 Luther _____ (fish) during his vacation time.

5 Hannah _____ (tennis) with her cousin on Monday evenings.

---

37 ✓ CHECKLIST

⚙ "Go" and "play" ☐   **Aa** Sports ☐   🧩 Talking about sports ☐

38.1 HOBBIES AND PASTIMES

do puzzles

play cards

play chess

play board games

play computer games /
play video games

read

draw

write

paint

take photos

play a musical
instrument

walk / hike

cook

bake

sew

knit

watch television

watch a movie (US)
watch a film (UK)

see a play

play sport /
do exercise

go to the gym

do yoga

listen to music

go camping

go bird watching

go out for a meal

do the gardening

visit a museum /
art gallery

meet friends

go on vacation (US)
go on holiday (UK)

go sightseeing

go shopping

39 Free time

Adverbs of frequency show how often you do something, from something you do very frequently ("always") to something you don't do at all ("never").

⚙ **New language** Adverbs of frequency
Aa Vocabulary Pastimes
🧩 **New skill** Talking about your free time

39.1 VOCABULARY ADVERBS OF FREQUENCY

Use adverbs of frequency to say how often you do something. You normally put the adverb between the subject and the verb.

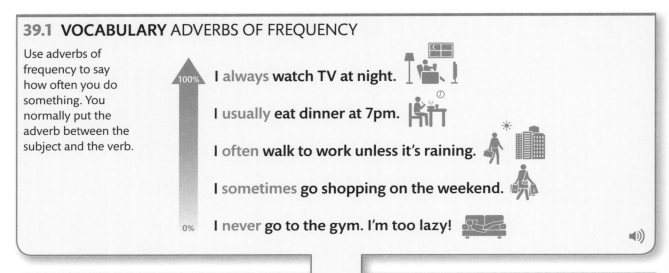

100%

I **always** watch TV at night.

I **usually** eat dinner at 7pm.

I **often** walk to work unless it's raining.

I **sometimes** go shopping on the weekend.

I **never** go to the gym. I'm too lazy!

0%

39.2 KEY LANGUAGE ADVERBS OF FREQUENCY

Time phrases often go at the ends of sentences using adverbs of frequency.

SUBJECT	ADVERB OF FREQUENCY	ACTIVITY	TIME PHRASE
I	always	watch TV	at night.

39.3 REWRITE THE SENTENCES, PUTTING THE WORDS IN THE CORRECT ORDER

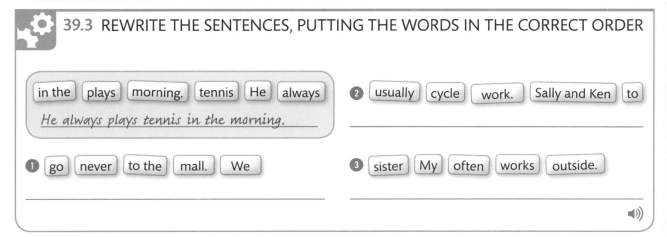

in the | plays | morning. | tennis | He | always

He always plays tennis in the morning.

❷ usually | cycle | work. | Sally and Ken | to

_____

❶ go | never | to the | mall. | We

_____

❸ sister | My | often | works | outside.

_____

136

39.4 LISTEN TO THE AUDIO AND MATCH THE PASTIME TO ITS FREQUENCY

Ben is taking part in a survey about how he spends his free time. Listen to his answers.

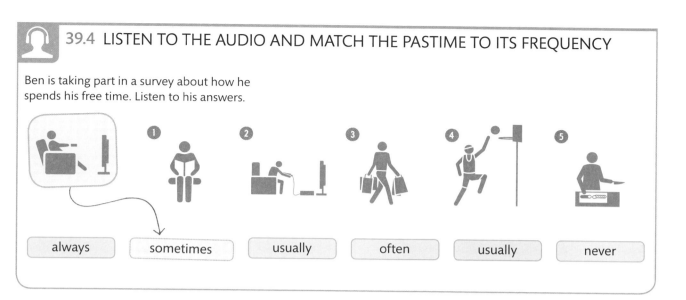

always   sometimes   usually   often   usually   never

39.5 LOOK AT THE TABLE AND SAY THE SENTENCES OUT LOUD, FILLING IN THE GAPS

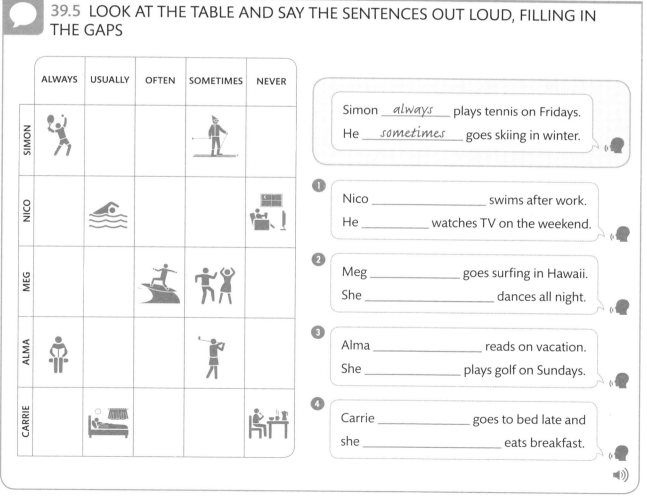

	ALWAYS	USUALLY	OFTEN	SOMETIMES	NEVER
SIMON	(tennis)			(skiing)	
NICO		(swimming)			(TV)
MEG			(surfing)	(dancing)	
ALMA	(cycling)			(golf)	
CARRIE		(sleeping)			(breakfast)

Simon ___always___ plays tennis on Fridays.
He ___sometimes___ goes skiing in winter.

① Nico _____ swims after work.
He _____ watches TV on the weekend.

② Meg _____ goes surfing in Hawaii.
She _____ dances all night.

③ Alma _____ reads on vacation.
She _____ plays golf on Sundays.

④ Carrie _____ goes to bed late and
she _____ eats breakfast.

39.6 HOW TO FORM QUESTIONS ABOUT FREE TIME

Use different phrases to ask about the frequency with which someone does an activity and the specific time that they do something.

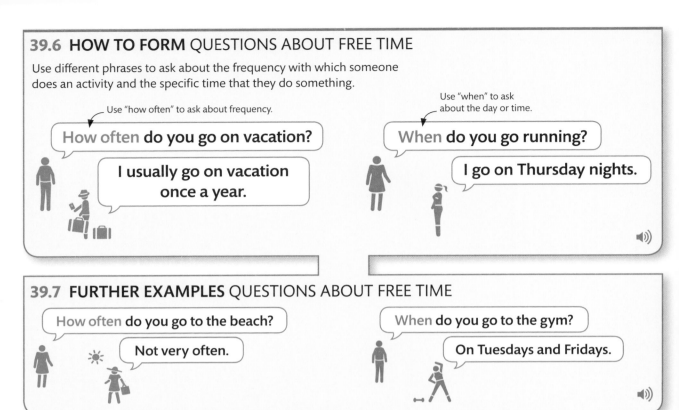

Use "how often" to ask about frequency.

How often do you go on vacation?

I usually go on vacation once a year.

Use "when" to ask about the day or time.

When do you go running?

I go on Thursday nights.

39.7 FURTHER EXAMPLES QUESTIONS ABOUT FREE TIME

How often do you go to the beach?

Not very often.

When do you go to the gym?

On Tuesdays and Fridays.

39.8 MARK THE CORRECT QUESTION FOR EACH ANSWER

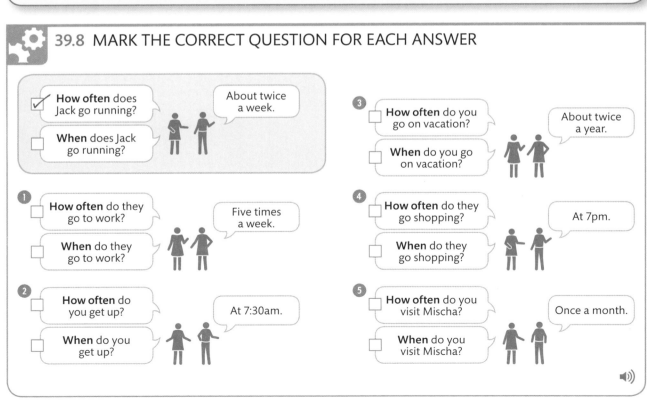

How often does Jack go running? ✓

When does Jack go running?

About twice a week.

① **How often** do they go to work?

When do they go to work?

Five times a week.

② **How often** do you get up?

When do you get up?

At 7:30am.

③ **How often** do you go on vacation?

When do you go on vacation?

About twice a year.

④ **How often** do they go shopping?

When do they go shopping?

At 7pm.

⑤ **How often** do you visit Mischa?

When do you visit Mischa?

Once a month.

39.9 WRITE A QUESTION BASED ON EACH STATEMENT USING "HOW OFTEN" OR "WHEN"

She goes dancing twice a week.
How often does she go dancing?

1 They visit their grandparents on Saturdays.

_____

2 We go skating during the winter.

_____

3 He usually plays hockey three times a month.

_____

4 You go shopping on Fridays.

_____

5 They see their parents every weekend.

_____

6 He never walks the dog.

_____

7 We sometimes go skating on the lake.

_____

39.10 SAY QUESTIONS OUT LOUD BASED ON THE STATEMENTS

How often do you listen to music?

I listen to music every night.

1 _____

I do yoga on Monday nights.

2 _____

I sometimes go to the movies.

3 _____

I go skateboarding three times a month.

4 _____

I arrive at work at 8am.

5 _____

I usually go surfing once a week.

40 Likes and dislikes

Verbs such as "love," "like," and "hate" express your feelings about things. You can use these verbs with nouns or gerunds.

⚙ **New language** "Love," "like," and "hate"
Aa **Vocabulary** Food, sports, and pastimes
🧩 **New skill** Talking about what you like

40.1 KEY LANGUAGE LIKES AND DISLIKES WITH NOUNS

You can use these verbs to talk about nouns.

Use "do not" or "don't" and "does not" or "doesn't" to make negative statements.

TIP
"Don't like" means "dislike," but people use "don't like" more often in spoken English.

She likes **tennis**.

Max doesn't like **pizza**.

I love **chocolate**.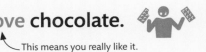
— This means you really like it.

They hate **coffee**.
— This is stronger than "don't like."

40.2 FURTHER EXAMPLES LIKES AND DISLIKES WITH NOUNS

I love **fries**.

You don't like **baseball**.

The cat doesn't like **its food**.

Oliver hates **board games**.

40.3 MATCH THE PICTURES TO THE CORRECT SENTENCES

Shania hates mice.

Sam doesn't like TV.

Ava and Elsa love the mountains.

Cats don't like the rain.

Manuel likes his book.

40.4 WRITE THE NEGATIVE OF EACH SENTENCE USING "DOESN'T" OR "DON'T"

Jack likes London. | *Jack doesn't like London.*

1. Imelda hates pasta.
2. My dog loves steak.
3. Our grandfather likes coffee.
4. I love the sea.
5. Sam and Jen hate hockey.
6. You like the countryside.
7. We like our new cell phones.

40.5 LISTEN TO THE AUDIO AND MARK THE CORRECT ANSWERS

Anna talks on Radio Chat about what she likes and dislikes.

Anna likes Matt's...
hat ☐ glasses. ☑

1. She doesn't like...
hockey ☐ golf. ☐

2. Anna likes...
some actors ☐ all actors. ☐

3. She loves...
pizza ☐ pasta. ☐

4. She doesn't like...
spiders ☐ snakes. ☐

40.6 USE THE CHART TO CREATE NINE CORRECT SENTENCES AND SAY THEM OUT LOUD

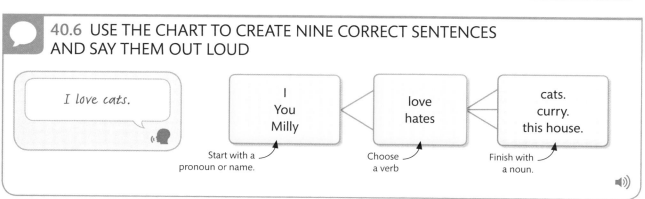

I love cats.

| I / You / Milly | love / hates | cats. / curry. / this house. |

Start with a pronoun or name.

Choose a verb

Finish with a noun.

40.7 KEY LANGUAGE LIKES AND DISLIKES WITH GERUNDS

You can use verbs such as "like" and "hate" with gerunds to talk about activities.

They like **playing chess.**

Ed doesn't like **cycling.**

I love **swimming.**

She hates **shopping.**

40.8 FURTHER EXAMPLES LIKES AND DISLIKES WITH GERUNDS

Vi and Lu love **playing golf.**

I don't like **working late.**

Elliot loves **watching birds.**

You like **drinking coffee.**

40.9 LISTEN TO THE AUDIO AND MATCH THE LIKES AND DISLIKES WITH THE CORRECT ACTIVITIES

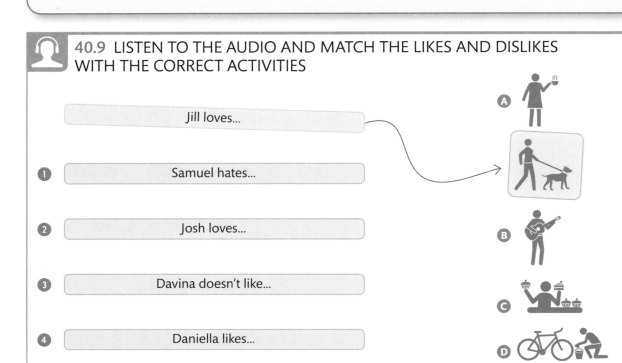

Jill loves...

1. Samuel hates...

2. Josh loves...

3. Davina doesn't like...

4. Daniella likes...

48 OLDTON NEWS

CLUBS AND SOCIETIES

An Oldton student tells us about some local clubs

I am Mark Watson and I'm at Oldton University. This is the first week of classes and students are trying lots of activities. This is what I think of them…

Chocolate Club: Do you like chocolate? Well, the people in this club love it! I don't like chocolate, so this club is not for me. They make chocolate cakes and chocolate drinks.

Dancing Club: My girlfriend loves this club. She goes twice a week. It is great exercise, but I hate it because I am very clumsy.

Computer Gaming Club: I love playing computer games at home. I really like playing with other people, too, so I like this club. There are lots of players there every week.

Chess Club: I love playing chess. I go to this club because it's a lot of fun. The players are very good, so I don't win very often. It makes me a better player.

Skateboarding Club: This is a fantastic club where you can learn from great skateboarders. This club meets three times a week and it's a great place to make new friends. I love it!

Mark loves chocolate.
True ☐ **False** ☑

1 People make cakes at Chocolate Club.
True ☐ **False** ☐

2 Mark's girlfriend hates dancing.
True ☐ **False** ☐

3 Mark likes dancing.
True ☐ **False** ☐

4 He loves computer games.
True ☐ **False** ☐

5 He doesn't like the chess club.
True ☐ **False** ☐

6 The players are very good.
True ☐ **False** ☐

7 Skateboarding Club is horrible.
True ☐ **False** ☐

8 Skateboarding Club meets three times a week.
True ☐ **False** ☐

9 Mark loves three of the clubs.
True ☐ **False** ☐

40.11 VOCABULARY REASONS FOR LIKES AND DISLIKES

You can use these adjectives to talk about why you like something.

exciting

interesting

tiring

fun

delicious

disgusting

boring

40.12 KEY LANGUAGE "DO" QUESTIONS ABOUT LIKES AND DISLIKES

Use "do" or "does" to ask if someone likes something.

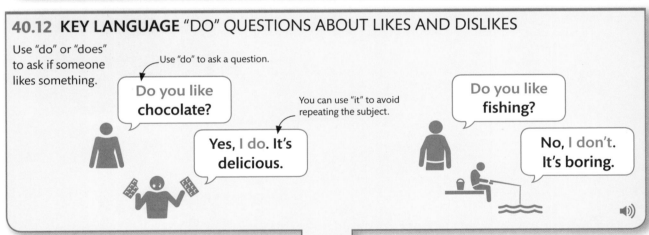

Use "do" to ask a question.

Do you like chocolate?

You can use "it" to avoid repeating the subject.

Yes, I do. It's delicious.

Do you like fishing?

No, I don't. It's boring.

40.13 KEY LANGUAGE "WHY" QUESTIONS ABOUT LIKES AND DISLIKES

You can use "why" to find out the reasons why someone likes or dislikes something.

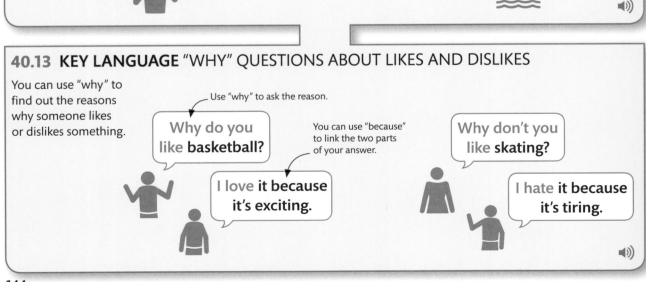

Use "why" to ask the reason.

Why do you like basketball?

You can use "because" to link the two parts of your answer.

I love it because it's exciting.

Why don't you like skating?

I hate it because it's tiring.

40.14 WRITE QUESTIONS BASED ON THE STATEMENTS

They hate football because it's boring.
Why do they hate football?

1 Una loves skiing because it's exciting.

_____

2 They like this book because it's interesting.

_____

3 Debbie doesn't like her job because it's boring.

_____

4 We don't like cooking.

_____

5 She loves surfing.

_____

6 I hate working late.

_____

7 Aziz loves Ontario.

_____

40.15 ANSWER THE QUESTIONS OUT LOUD, USING THE WORDS IN THE PANEL

Why do they like pasta?

They like pasta because _____ *it's delicious* _____.

1 Why do you like English class?

I like English class because _____.

2 Why do you love skating?

We love skating because _____.

3 Why does Luca hate cleaning?

He hates cleaning because _____.

it's exciting

~~it's delicious~~

it's boring

it's interesting

40 ✓ CHECKLIST

⚙ "Love," "like," and "hate" ☐   **Aa** Food, sports, and pastimes ☐   Talking about what you like ☐

145

41.1 MUSIC

classical music

hip-hop

jazz

country

opera

soul

rap

rock

pop

Latin

orchestra

band /group

play the trumpet

guitar player

concert

festival

sing a song

singer

headphones

album

dance

microphone

conductor

audience

41.2 MUSICAL INSTRUMENTS

guitar

electric guitar

piano

keyboard

violin

saxophone

harmonica

trumpet

drum

flute

42 Expressing preference

You use "like" and "love" to show how much you enjoy something. "Favorite" is used to identify the thing you love most in a group.

✿ **New language** Using "favorite"
Aa Vocabulary Food and music
🧩 **New skill** Talking about your favorite things

42.1 KEY LANGUAGE USING "FAVORITE"

"Like" and "love" are verbs, so they need subjects and objects. "Favorite" is an adjective, so it is always paired with a noun or gerund.

Remember, this verb is stronger than "like."

I like jazz and I love soul, but my favorite type of music is rock.

This shows you like this thing the most.

"Favorite" can be followed by a noun or the phrase "type of" and a noun.

42.2 FURTHER EXAMPLES USING "FAVORITE"

She likes salsa dancing.

Abdul loves sailing.

"Italian" is not a particular food, but a "type of" food.

Her favorite type of food is Italian.

Basketball is his favourite sport.

The UK spelling is "favourite".

42.3 LISTEN TO THE AUDIO AND ANSWER THE QUESTIONS

Martin's favorite type of music is...
soul ☐ jazz ☐ rock. ✓

1 His favorite type of sport is...
baseball ☐ basketball ☐ squash. ☐

2 His favorite food is...
fish ☐ chicken ☐ beef. ☐

3 His favorite city is...
Rome ☐ Sydney ☐ New York. ☐

4 His favorite job is being a...
gardener ☐ hairdresser ☐ waiter. ☐

5 His favorite type of food is...
Mexican ☐ Italian ☐ French. ☐

6 His favorite type of exercise is...
running ☐ cycling ☐ yoga. ☐

7 Martin and his girlfriend's favorite pastime is...
gardening ☐ cooking ☐ dancing. ☐

42.4 MARK THE PICTURE THAT MATCHES EACH STATEMENT

Jack's **favorite** music is jazz.

Ⓐ ☐ Ⓑ ☑ Ⓒ ☐

❶ Ava's **favorite** thing is her new dress.

Ⓐ ☐ Ⓑ ☐ Ⓒ ☐

❷ Deborah's **favorite** pet is her dog.

Ⓐ ☐ Ⓑ ☐ Ⓒ ☐

❸ Aman's **favorite** sport is hockey.

Ⓐ ☐ Ⓑ ☐ Ⓒ ☐

❹ Mo and Jamie's **favorite** food is chocolate.

Ⓐ ☐ Ⓑ ☐ Ⓒ ☐

❺ Atif's **favorite** city is New York.

Ⓐ ☐ Ⓑ ☐ Ⓒ ☐

42.5 FILL IN THE GAPS USING THE WORDS IN THE PANEL

Dana's favorite type of music is _____*opera*_____.

❶ Grace's favorite food is _____.

❷ Poppy's favorite sport is _____.

❸ Dylan's favorite animal is his _____.

❹ Justin's favorite country is _____.

❺ Ling's favorite pastime is _____.

❻ Abdul's favorite color is _____.

❼ Mira's favorite number is _____.

❽ Jacob's favorite sweater is _____.

❾ Tori's favorite relative is her _____.

| surfing | ~~opera~~ | cousin | horse | pizza | 10 |
| Australia | knitting | purple | woolen | |

🔊

149

42.6 LOOK AT THESE ONLINE PROFILES, THEN FILL IN THE GAPS AND SAY THE SENTENCES OUT LOUD

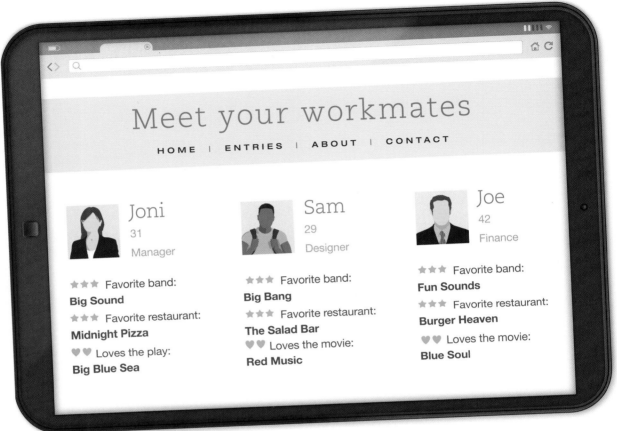

Meet your workmates

HOME | ENTRIES | ABOUT | CONTACT

Joni
31
Manager

★★★ Favorite band:
Big Sound
★★★ Favorite restaurant:
Midnight Pizza
♥♥ Loves the play:
Big Blue Sea

Sam
29
Designer

★★★ Favorite band:
Big Bang
★★★ Favorite restaurant:
The Salad Bar
♥♥ Loves the movie:
Red Music

Joe
42
Finance

★★★ Favorite band:
Fun Sounds
★★★ Favorite restaurant:
Burger Heaven
♥♥ Loves the movie:
Blue Soul

Joni's favorite band is ____*Big Sound*____.

4 Sam's favorite restaurant is _____.

1 Sam's _____ Big Bang.

5 Joe's _____ Burger Heaven.

2 Joe's favorite band is _____.

6 Joni _____ called Big Blue Sea.

3 Joni's _____ Midnight Pizza.

7 Joe loves the movie called _____.

42.7 READ THE ARTICLE AND ANSWER THE QUESTIONS

What is the favorite time to exercise?

morning ☑ **afternoon** ☐ **evening** ☐

1 What type of exercise is their favorite?

yoga ☐ **running** ☐ **swimming** ☐

2 What is Stanton people's favorite type of food?

pizza ☐ **burgers** ☐ **ice cream** ☐

3 What is their favorite sport?

golf ☐ **football** ☐ **surfing** ☐

4 Their favorite night out is going to...

the movies ☐ **the theater** ☐ **a restaurant.** ☐

STANTON REVIEW

Town favorites

What's your favorite time to exercise? The morning, the afternoon, or the evening? In Stanton, people say it's the morning because there are too many other things to do in the evening. The favorite exercise is yoga: 20 classes take place each week.

Stanton townspeople like food. They eat lots of it: 4,000,000 burgers, 2,000,000 pizzas, and 3,000,000 ice cream cones every year.

And how about sports? In Stanton, there are hundreds of golfers and football players, but the favorite sport is surfing.

People like going out in the evening. Many love movies and the theater, but that's not their favorite night out. It's dinner in a restaurant. Food again. That's not a surprise!

---

42 ✓ CHECKLIST

⚙ Using "favorite" ☐   **Aa** Food and music ☐   🧩 Talking about your favorite things ☐

♻ REVIEW THE ENGLISH YOU HAVE LEARNED IN UNITS 37–42

NEW LANGUAGE	SAMPLE SENTENCE	☑	UNIT
"GO" WITH GERUNDS, "PLAY" WITH NOUNS	I go swimming **on Mondays** and I play tennis **with my brother on Fridays.**	☐	37.1, 37.7
ADVERBS OF FREQUENCY	I always watch TV **at night,** and I sometimes go the the movies.	☐	39.1
QUESTIONS ABOUT FREE TIME	How often do you **go on vacation?** When does she **go running?**	☐	39.6
LIKES AND DISLIKES	She likes **tennis.** Max doesn't like **pizza.** I love **swimming.** She hates **shopping.**	☐	40.1, 40.7
QUESTIONS ABOUT LIKES AND DISLIKES	Do you like **chocolate?** Why do you like **basketball?**	☐	40.12, 40.13
USING "FAVORITE"	My favorite type of **music is rock.**	☐	42.1

43 Vocabulary

43.1 ABILITIES

jump

climb

fly

ride

drive

play

kick

throw

hit

catch

see

listen

whisper

talk

speak

shout

carry

make (a snowman)

do (homework)

think

act

remember

understand

spell

sit

stand up

walk

move

lift

work

add

subtract

Use "can" to talk about the things you are able to do, such as ride a bicycle or play the guitar. Use "cannot" or "can't" for things you are not able to do.

⚙ **New language** "Can," "can't," and "cannot"

Aa Vocabulary Talents and abilities

New skill Saying what you can and can't do

44.1 KEY LANGUAGE "CAN / CANNOT / CAN'T"

"Can" goes between the subject and the verb. The verb after "can" changes to its base form (the infinitive without "to").

I can ride a bicycle.

└ Base form of verb.

He can play the guitar.

└ "Can" is always the same.
It doesn't change with the subject.

TIP
The long negative form "cannot" is always spelled as one word, not two words.

I { cannot / can't } sing jazz songs.

└ Short form of "cannot."

🔊

44.2 FURTHER EXAMPLES "CAN / CANNOT / CAN'T"

Janet can play tennis.

He cannot climb the tree.

Bob can swim well.

They can't lift the box.

🔊

44.3 HOW TO FORM "CAN / CANNOT / CAN'T"

SUBJECT	"CAN / CANNOT / CAN'T"	BASE FORM	OBJECT
She	can cannot can't	ride	a bicycle.

44.4 REWRITE THE SENTENCES, PUTTING THE WORDS IN THE CORRECT ORDER

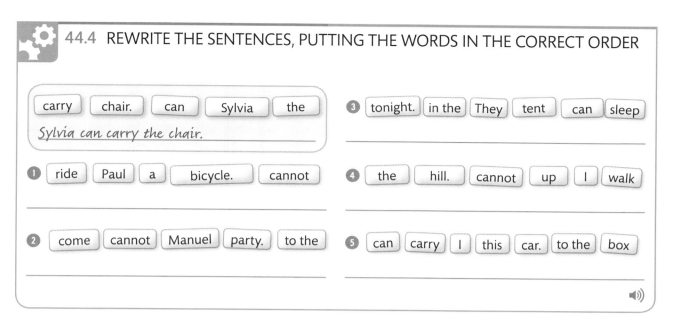

carry · chair. · can · Sylvia · the

Sylvia can carry the chair.

❶ ride · Paul · a · bicycle. · cannot

_____

❷ come · cannot · Manuel · party. · to the

_____

❸ tonight. · in the · They · tent · can · sleep

_____

❹ the · hill. · cannot · up · I · walk

_____

❺ can · carry · I · this · car. · to the · box

_____

44.5 CROSS OUT THE INCORRECT WORD IN EACH SENTENCE

My son is sick. He ~~can~~ / can't go to school today.

❶ Jo's pen doesn't work. She can / can't write her letter.

❷ I understand the homework, so I can / can't do it.

❸ The museum is closed. We can / can't get in.

❹ I have the car today, so I can / can't drive you.

❺ It's cold outside, so we can / can't have a picnic.

❻ Tony needs to work late, so he can / can't come.

❼ We can / can't play tennis. It's too dark.

44.6 FILL IN THE GAPS TO WRITE EACH SENTENCE THREE DIFFERENT WAYS

I can read Russian.	I cannot read Russian.	I can't read Russian.
❶ _____	Shirley cannot drive a car.	_____
❷ Ben and Julie can carry boxes.	_____	_____
❸ _____	_____	Ilaria can't spell English words.
❹ _____	He cannot go to work.	_____

44.7 KEY LANGUAGE QUESTIONS AND SHORT ANSWERS

To make a question using "can," put "can" before the subject. When you answer "can" questions, you don't need to repeat all the words from the question.

Can you **ride a bicycle**?

Yes, I can.

No, I can't.

44.8 FURTHER EXAMPLES QUESTIONS AND SHORT ANSWERS

Can she **speak Japanese**?

Yes, she can.

Can we **climb that mountain**?

No, we can't.

Can they **swim**?

No, they can't.

Can you **move that chair**?

Yes, I can.

44.9 SAY THE SENTENCES OUT LOUD, FILLING IN THE GAPS

Can you lift that heavy box?

Yes, _____I can._____

① Can he play the piano?

No, _____

② Can they catch that big fish?

Yes, _____

③ Can you hit that ball over there?

No, _____

④ Can you spell "excited?"

Yes, _____

⑤ Can we lift this big table?

No, _____

⑥ Can she fly a kite in this weather?

Yes, _____

⑦ Can they cycle into town?

No, _____

156

44.10 WRITE QUESTIONS TO MATCH THE STATEMENTS

Paul and Mary can speak Chinese.
Can Paul and Mary speak Chinese?

❶ The dog can jump over the wall.

_____

❷ Denise can touch her toes.

_____

❸ I can lift my son onto my shoulders.

_____

❹ Grandma can see the TV.

_____

❺ I can hit the tennis ball over the net.

_____

◀))

44.11 LISTEN TO THE AUDIO AND ANSWER THE QUESTIONS

Sheila and Mark talk about the things they can and can't cook.

Sheila can make a salad.
True ✓ **False** ☐

❶ Sheila doesn't eat meat.
True ☐ **False** ☐

❷ Mark can't cook a roast chicken.
True ☐ **False** ☐

❸ Sheila and Mark can both cook vegetables.
True ☐ **False** ☐

❹ Sheila can make an apple pie.
True ☐ **False** ☐

44.12 FILL IN THE GAPS WITH "CAN" OR "CANNOT"

Janet is a chef. She ___ _can_ ___ cook very well.

❶ Paul and Jerry don't like the ocean because they _____ swim.

❷ I ride my bike to work because I _____ drive.

❸ Jim cannot climb over the wall, but he _____ walk around it.

❹ My mother _____ lift that bag because it's too heavy.

❺ My sister Penny loves music and _____ dance to any song.

◀))

45 Describing actions

Words such as "quietly" and "loudly" are called adverbs. They give more information about verbs, so you can use them to describe how you do something.

🔧 **New language** Regular and irregular adverbs
Aa Vocabulary Hobbies and activities
🧩 **New skill** Describing activities

45.1 KEY LANGUAGE USING ADVERBS

Adverbs often come after the verb they describe.

"Quietly" describes how I speak.

I speak quietly.
He speaks loudly.

"Loudly" describes how he speaks.

Hello. HELLO!

45.2 FURTHER EXAMPLES USING ADVERBS

A tortoise moves slowly.

Horses can run quickly.

She sings beautifully.

I can play the piano badly.

45.3 FILL IN THE GAPS USING THE WORDS IN THE PANEL

 Tommy plays the guitar ___*badly*___ .

 ① Mary can speak French _____ .

② Roger can run very _____ .

 ③ The old man walks _____ .

④ He talks very _____ .

⑤ She won the race _____ .

| excellently | ~~badly~~ | loudly | quickly | easily | slowly |

158

45.4 KEY LANGUAGE REGULAR AND IRREGULAR ADVERBS

REGULAR ADVERBS

To make most adverbs, just add "-ly" to the adjective. If the adjective ends in "y," leave out the "y" and add "-ily" to make the adverb.

bad → **bad**ly

careful → **careful**ly

easy → **eas**ily
Drop the "y" and add "-ily."

IRREGULAR ADVERBS

Some adverbs are totally different to the adjective. Others are the same. These are called irregular adverbs.

good → well
The adverb is totally different to the adjective.

hard → hard
The adverb is the same as the adjective.

early → early
Adjectives ending "-ly" don't change to become adverbs.

Aa 45.5 FIND 8 ADVERBS AND WRITE THEM IN THE CORRECT COLUMN

```
E A S I L Y W L K Q G
B N O Y U T E O A U R
A J S L O X L S G I W
D F L O U D L Y T C E
L F H A B L W H F K M
Y A G A R U E A R L Y
C S F U S Y Q R V Y W
I T R S L K A D B M S
```

REGULAR

1 Loudly

2 _____

3 _____

4 _____

IRREGULAR

5 Fast

6 _____

7 _____

8 _____

45.6 REWRITE THE SENTENCES, CORRECTING THE ERRORS

My friend John walks very quick.
My friend John walks very quickly.

1 You speak English very good.

_____

2 Damian cooks burgers bad.

_____

3 I can get to your house easy.

_____

4 Benjy always listens careful.

_____

5 My brother always works hardly.

_____

6 Sammy always plays his guitar loud.

_____

45.7 ANOTHER WAY TO SAY I DO SOMETHING WELL

If you're "good at" doing something, you do it well. Use a gerund or nouns after the phrase to say what you're "good at."

She can run well.

She's good at running.

You can use the gerund after "good at."

45.8 HOW TO FORM "GOOD AT / BAD AT"

The negative form of "good at" is "bad at."

SUBJECT + VERB	"GOOD AT / BAD AT"	GERUND / NOUN
She's	good at bad at	skiing. English.

45.9 FURTHER EXAMPLES "GOOD AT / BAD AT"

 Aziz is good at climbing trees.

 I am bad at making cakes.

 Kate is good at soccer.

 Harris is bad at chess.

45.10 REWRITE THE SENTENCES, PUTTING THE WORDS IN THE CORRECT ORDER

| the guitar. | good at | playing | Pablo is |

Pablo is good at playing the guitar.

1 | is | at | good | My horse | jumping. |

_____

2 | bad at | early. | getting up | I am |

_____

3 | writing | Mary is | bad at | German. |

_____

4 | good | swimming. | at | are | Jo and Bob |

_____

5 | cleaning. | is | Millie | bad at |

_____

45.11 REWRITE EACH SENTENCE IN ITS OTHER FORM

> She can play the piano well.
> _She's good at playing the piano._

① Conchita can play basketball well.

_____

② You're good at driving a van.

_____

③ Shania and Dave can surf well.

_____

④ My father is bad at speaking English.

_____

⑤ Manu can't write stories well.

_____

45.12 LISTEN TO THE AUDIO AND MARK WHO IS GOOD AT OR BAD AT EACH ACTIVITY

Good at ✔ Bad at ☐

① Good at ☐ Bad at ☐

② Good at ☐ Bad at ☐

③ Good at ☐ Bad at ☐

④ Good at ☐ Bad at ☐

45.13 USE THE CHART TO CREATE 12 CORRECT SENTENCES AND SAY THEM OUT LOUD

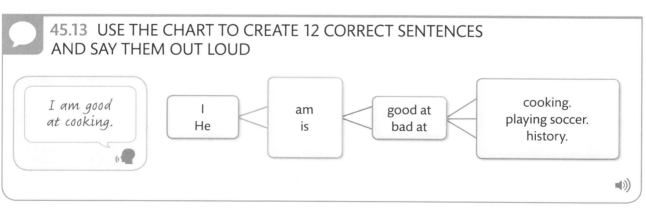

I am good at cooking.

| I / He | am / is | good at / bad at | cooking. / playing soccer. / history. |

45 ✓ CHECKLIST

⚙ Regular and irregular adverbs ☐   **Aa** Hobbies and activities ☐   🧩 Describing activities ☐

46 Describing ability

Words such as "quite" and "very" are modifying adverbs. You can use them before other adverbs to give more information about how you do something.

⚙ **New language** Modifying adverbs
Aa Vocabulary Skills and abilities
🧩 **New skill** Saying how well you do things

46.1 KEY LANGUAGE MODIFYING ADVERBS

If you do something "quite" well, you're OK but not excellent at it. If you do it "very" or "really" well, you're excellent.

"Quite" modifies the main adverb, "well," and goes before it.

I can ski quite well.

She can ski { very / really } well.

TIP
In US English, "quite" is used to add emphasis to an adverb.

46.2 FURTHER EXAMPLES MODIFYING ADVERBS

Ben can climb really high.

Jenny can swim very well.

My dad dances quite well.

I speak Spanish quite well.

Aa 46.3 MATCH THE BEGINNING OF THE SENTENCES TO THE CORRECT ENDINGS

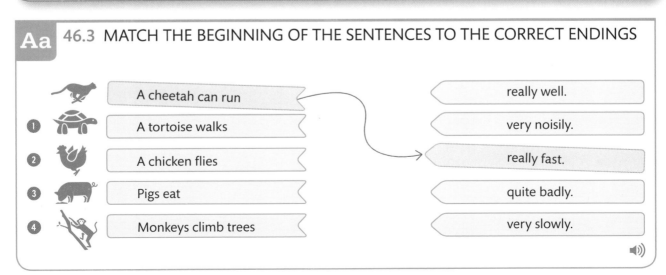

A cheetah can run — really fast.

1. A tortoise walks — very noisily.

2. A chicken flies — really well.

3. Pigs eat — quite badly.

4. Monkeys climb trees — very slowly.

46.4 KEY LANGUAGE MODIFYING ADVERBS WITH "GOOD AT"

You can also use modifying adverbs with the phrases "good at" and "bad at."

She can play golf quite well.

She's quite good at playing golf.

"Quite" modifies "good at."

Remember that "good at" and "bad at" are followed by a gerund.

You can play golf { very / really } well.

You're { very / really } good at playing golf.

"Very / really" goes before "good at."

46.5 READ THE REPORT AND ANSWER THE QUESTIONS

How good is Juan at learning vocabulary?
Quite good ✓   **Really good** ☐

1 How good is he at speaking English?
Quite good ☐   **Really good** ☐

2 How good is Juan at reading?
Quite good ☐   **Really good** ☐

3 How good is he at listening to English?
Quite good ☐   **Really good** ☐

4 How good is Juan at writing English?
Quite good ☐   **Really good** ☐

English report: Juan Ramirez

Writing 99%	Excellent.
Vocabulary 65%	Ok, but you need to study more.
Speaking 95%	Well done.
Listening 66%	Better. Try watching more English movies to improve.
Reading 63%	Ok. You need to read more English texts to improve.

---

46 ✓ CHECKLIST

⚙ Modifying adverbs ☐   **Aa** Skills and abilities ☐   🧩 Saying how well you do things ☐

47 Wishes and desires

You can use "I want" and "I would like" to talk about things you want to do. You can also use their negative form to say what you would not like to do.

⚙ **New language** "Would" and "want"
Aa Vocabulary Leisure activities
🧩 **New skill** Talking about ambitions

47.1 KEY LANGUAGE "I WOULD LIKE / I WANT"

"I would like" is similar to "I want," but "I want" is stronger.

He wants to write a book.

He has a strong desire to do a thing.

I would like to climb a mountain.

I'd like to go scuba diving.

The contracted form of "I would."

47.2 HOW TO FORM "I WOULD LIKE / I'D LIKE"

"Would" is a modal verb, so its form doesn't change.

SUBJECT	MODAL VERB	VERB	INFINITIVE + OBJECT
I / You / He / She We / You / They	would	like	to go cycling.

47.3 FURTHER EXAMPLES "I'D LIKE / I WANT"

She'd like **to go to Bali.**

We'd like **to cook dinner.**

I'd like **to drive a sports car.**

He wants **to go surfing in Hawaii.**

We want **to go on a boat.**

The dog wants **to jump in the river.**

47.4 FILL IN THE GAPS TO WRITE EACH SENTENCE THREE DIFFERENT WAYS

I want to buy a house.	*I would like to buy a house.*	*I'd like to buy a house.*
❶ _____	_____	He'd like to get a dog.
❷ _____	You would like to work in Turkey.	_____
❸ We want to learn Chinese.	_____	_____
❹ _____	_____	They'd like to start a rock band.

Aa 47.5 MATCH THE PICTURES TO THE DESCRIPTIONS

He'd like to travel around Asia.	He'd like to act in a musical.	He wants to be in the Olympics.	She wants to work with lions in Africa.	She'd like to sail a boat.

🔊

47.6 USE THE CHART TO CREATE 12 CORRECT SENTENCES AND SAY THEM OUT LOUD

I'd like to climb this tree.

I'd like / I want / She wants	to climb / to read	this tree. / that mountain. / a newspaper. / another book.

🔊

47.7 KEY LANGUAGE "I WOULD LIKE / I WANT" NEGATIVES

Use "not" after "would" to make the negative. "Don't" and "doesn't" go before "want."

I would not like **to go snowboarding.**

I wouldn't like **to go shopping.**

The contracted form of "would not."

They don't want **to go fishing.**

"Don't" goes before "want."

47.8 FURTHER EXAMPLES "I WOULD LIKE / I WANT" NEGATIVES

They wouldn't like **to go swimming.**

We don't want **to eat dinner.**

She wouldn't like **to be a hairdresser.**

He doesn't want **to go shopping.**

47.9 FILL IN THE GAPS TO WRITE EACH SENTENCE THREE DIFFERENT WAYS

I would not like to go skiing.	I wouldn't like to go skiing.	I don't want to go skiing.
❶ _____	_____	He doesn't want to play tennis.
❷ _____	She wouldn't like to study science.	_____
❸ _____	_____	They don't want to go to work.
❹ You would not like to sing.	_____	_____
❺ _____	We wouldn't like to go diving.	_____

47.10 KEY LANGUAGE QUESTIONS AND SHORT ANSWERS

"Would" goes before the subject in a question.

Would you like **to play chess?** Yes, I would.

Does he want **to go to the movies?** Yes, he does.

"Does" goes before the subject in questions with "want."

47.11 LISTEN TO THE AUDIO AND ANSWER THE QUESTIONS

Does Mark want to play tennis later?
Yes, he does. ✓ **No, he doesn't.** ☐

① Would Sarah like to go to a restaurant today?
Yes, she would. ☐ **No, she wouldn't.** ☐

② Does Vangelis want to make the dinner?
Yes, he does. ☐ **No, he doesn't.** ☐

③ Would Lee like to work on Saturday?
Yes, he would. ☐ **No, he wouldn't.** ☐

④ Does Mary want to skateboard tonight?
Yes, she does. ☐ **No, she doesn't.** ☐

⑤ Would Anoushka like to go bowling?
Yes, she would. ☐ **No, she wouldn't.** ☐

47.12 REWRITE THE SENTENCES, CORRECTING THE ERRORS

Would you **want** to go home?
Would you like to go home?

① He **don't** want to climb that hill.

_____

② I wouldn't **likes** to be a judge.

_____

③ They **doesn't** want to go to work today.

_____

④ She would **want** to play tennis tonight.

_____

⑤ I **wants** to climb that tree.

_____

47 ✓ CHECKLIST

⚙ "Would" and "want" ☐   **Aa** Leisure activities ☐   🧩 Talking about ambitions ☐

167

48 Studying

When talking about your studies you can use "I would" and "I want" to say which subjects you would like to learn. Use adverbs to say how much you want to do them.

⚙ **New language** Adverbs and articles
Aa Vocabulary Academic subjects
🧩 **New skill** Talking about your studies

48.1 VOCABULARY ACADEMIC SUBJECTS

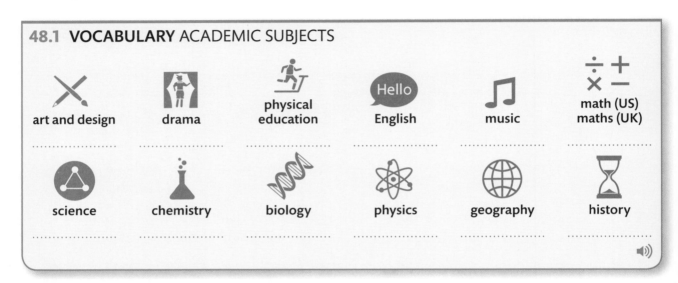

art and design

drama

physical education

English

music

math (US) maths (UK)

science

chemistry

biology

physics

geography

history

48.2 KEY LANGUAGE "REALLY / QUITE"

The adverb "really" means you want to do something a lot. "Quite" is less strong.

I love music. I'd **really** like to study it next term.

└ You have a strong desire to do it.

I like biology. I'd **quite** like to study it next year.

└ Your desire is not as strong.

48.3 FURTHER EXAMPLES "REALLY / QUITE"

Bella is good at science, and she'd **really** like to study it at college.

Richard loves jazz, so he'd **really** like to go to that music festival.

This band is OK. I'd **quite** like to listen to their new CD.

48.4 VOCABULARY STUDYING

learn
....

practice (US)
practise (UK)
....

take an exam
....

pass an exam
....

get a degree
....

🔊

48.5 REWRITE THE SENTENCES, PUTTING THE WORDS IN THE CORRECT ORDER

| to do | quite | an English degree. | like | Sheila | would |

Sheila would quite like to do an English degree.

1 | his driving test. | Jerry | really | would | to pass | like |

_____

2 | would | an IELTS test. | like | Ben and Sam | to take | really |

_____

3 | like | Helen | her English. | would | to practice | quite |

_____

4 | the piano | like | quite | to play | tonight. | I'd |

_____

🔊

48.6 USE THE CHART TO CREATE 12 CORRECT SENTENCES AND SAY THEM OUT LOUD

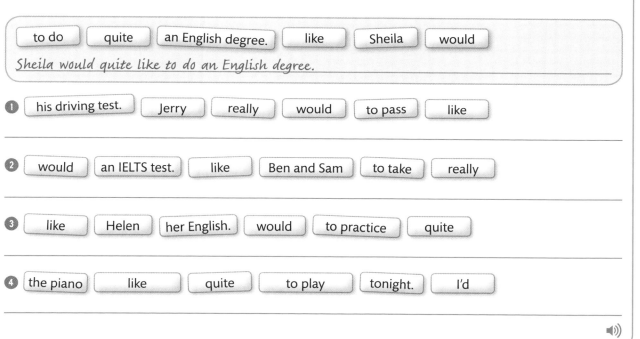

I'd really like to practice my spelling.

| I'd / Laila would | really / quite | like | to practice my spelling. / to pass her history exam. / to do a biology degree. / to learn English. |

🔊

48.7 KEY LANGUAGE THE ZERO ARTICLE

You don't use an article ("a" or "the") with some places and institutions when you are talking about what they are used for.

She goes there to study, which is the purpose of schools, so don't use the article.

Liz is seven. She goes to school now.

Larry works at the school in Park Street.

Use the article to talk about the specific building where he works.

48.8 FURTHER EXAMPLES THE ZERO ARTICLE

ZERO ARTICLE

I am at university in Chicago.

Pierre is in hospital.

Liz goes to church on Sundays.

Go to bed, Tom!

Sue is in town this afternoon.

Sarah studies at home.

ARTICLE

The University of Chicago is good.

The hospital is far away.

St. Mary's is an old church.

Your shirt is on the bed.

Hancock is a nice town.

This dog hasn't got a home.

48.9 CROSS OUT THE INCORRECT WORDS IN EACH SENTENCE

Sheila works at ~~school~~ / the school near here.

① Emily has **lovely home** / a lovely home.

② Sue always takes her lunch to **office** / the office.

③ Can you see where **church** / the church is?

④ Jim went to **bed** / the bed hours ago.

⑤ Can you drive me into **town** / a town later?

⑥ I live next to **university** / the university.

⑦ I leave **home** / a home at 8am every weekday.

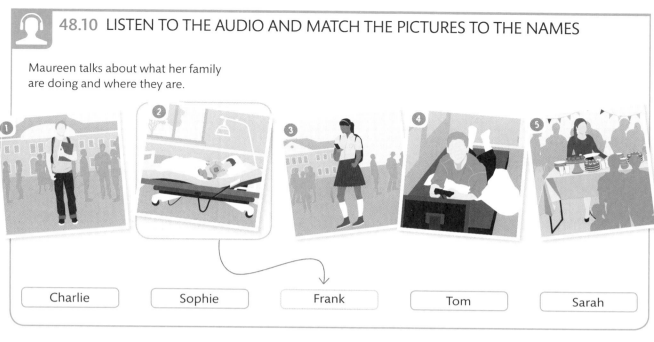

48.10 LISTEN TO THE AUDIO AND MATCH THE PICTURES TO THE NAMES

Maureen talks about what her family are doing and where they are.

Charlie | Sophie | Frank | Tom | Sarah

48 ✓ CHECKLIST

⚙ Adverbs and articles ☐   **Aa** Academic subjects ☐   🧩 Talking about your studies ☐

♻ REVIEW THE ENGLISH YOU HAVE LEARNED IN UNITS 44-48

NEW LANGUAGE	SAMPLE SENTENCE	☑	UNIT
"CAN," "CANNOT," AND "CAN'T"	I can ride a bicycle. He can play guitar. I cannot / can't sing jazz songs.	☐	44.1, 44.3, 44.7
USING ADVERBS	I speak quietly. He speaks loudly.	☐	45.1, 45.4
"GOOD AT" AND "BAD AT"	She's good at running. I am bad at making cakes.	☐	45.7, 45.8
MODIFYING ADVERBS	I can ski quite well. She can ski very well. She can ski really well.	☐	46.1, 46.4
"I WOULD LIKE" AND "I WANT"	He wants to write a book. I would like to climb a mountain.	☐	47.1, 47.7
"REALLY" AND "QUITE"	I love music. I'd really like to study it this term. I like biology. I'd quite like to study it next year.	☐	48.2, 48.3
THE ZERO ARTICLE	My daughter goes to school now.	☐	48.7, 48.8

Answers

1.4 ◀))
1. I'm Charlotte.
2. My name's Una.
3. My name's Simone.
4. I'm Carlos.
5. I'm Juan.
6. My name's Miriam.
7. I'm Sarah.

1.5
A) 5
B) 1
C) 2
D) 3
E) 6
F) 4

1.6 ◀))
1. Hi! My name is Linda.
2. Hi! My name is Abdul.
3. Hi! My name is Paolo.
4. Hello! My name is Linda.
5. Hello! My name is Abdul.
6. Hello! My name is Paolo.
7. Hi! I am Linda.
8. Hi! I am Abdul.
9. Hi! I am Paolo.
10. Hello! I am Linda.
11. Hello! I am Abdul.
12. Hello! I am Paolo.

1.9
1. B-E-L-I-N-D-A
2. L-E-W-I-S
3. A-D-A-M-S
4. B-O-B
5. S-P-E-N-C-E-R
6. K-A-T-E W-A-L-L-A-C-E
7. S-A-U-L J-A-C-K-S-O-N
8. N-A-T-A-L-I-E L-A-U
9. C-H-R-I-S B-O-Y-L-E

1.10 ◀))
1. B-A-S-H-I-R
2. B-E-N J-A-M-E-S
3. M-O-L-L-Y
4. L-O-P-E-Z
5. N-A-D-I-Y-A L-A-T-I-F

3.5 ◀))
1. eleven
2. seventeen
3. thirty-four
4. fifty-nine
5. eighty-five

3.6 ◀))
1. Theo **is** 45 years old.
2. Madison **is** 27 years old.
3. Jeremy and Tanya **are** 90 years old.
4. We **are** 29 years old.
5. I **am** 34 years old.

3.8
1. 40
2. 30
3. 19
4. 60
5. 80
6. 17
7. 13

3.12
1. Japan
2. US
3. France

3.13 ◀))
1. Spanish
2. German
3. Canadian
4. American
5. Australian
6. Chinese

3.14 ◀))
1. I am Australian.
2. I am English.
3. I am from Italy.
4. I am from France.
5. You are Australian.
6. You are English.
7. You are from Italy.
8. You are from France.
9. They are Australian.
10. They are English.
11. They are from Italy.
12. They are from France.

5.3 ◀))
1. your horse
2. their sheep
3. our fish

4. its bone
5. his dog

5.4 ◀))
1. Bingo is **my** dog.
2. **Her** aunt is called Goldie.
3. **My** cat eats fish.
4. **Their** rabbit lives in the backyard.
5. **Our** parrot is from Colombia.
6. **His** wife is called Henrietta.
7. **Their** dog is 10 years old.
8. **Our** aunt lives on a farm in Ohio.
9. Here is **its** ball.

5.5 ◀))
1. Farida **is** their sister.
2. Duke **is** our dog.
3. Daisy **is** her mother.
4. They **are** his grandparents.
5. It **is** our horse.
6. John **is** our cousin.
7. I **am** Daisy's daughter.
8. You **are** my friend.

5.8 ◀))
1. **This** is her horse.
2. **That** is our rabbit.
3. **That** is their pig.
4. **This** is his cow.
5. **This** is your fish.

5.9 ◀))
1. Lily is their sister.
2. Our son is 12 years old.
3. That is their cow.
4. This is your ball.
5. Her father is called Caspar.

5.10
A) 2
B) 1
C) 5
D) 3
E) 4

5.11 ◀))
1. This is my cat.
2. This is my parrot.
3. This is her cat.
4. This is her parrot.
5. This is their cat.
6. This is their parrot.
7. That is my cat.
8. That is my parrot.
9. That is her cat.
10. That is her parrot.
11. That is their cat.
12. That is their parrot.

06

6.3 🔊
1. Ben's son
2. Sam and Ayshah's cat
3. Debbie's house
4. Marco and Kate's car
5. Elsa's grandchild
6. Beth's parrot

6.4
1. Lucas is Ben's father.
2. Lily is Ben's mother.
3. Noah is Ben's son.
4. Grace is Ben's sister.
5. Alex is Ben's brother.

6.7 🔊
1. Angela is Skanda's wife.
2. That is my cousins' snake.
3. Sue is Ella and Mark's aunt.
4. Ginger is John's cat.

6.8 🔊
1. Kathy is **Dave's** aunt.
2. Rex is **Noah and Pat's** dog.
3. This is **her cousins'** house.
4. Felix is **the children's** cat.

08

8.2 🔊
1. **These** are Diego's keys.
2. **This** is Olivia's purse.
3. **Those** are my books.
4. **These** are my pencils.
5. **That** is Anna's sandwich.
6. **That** is Malik's phone.

8.3
1. That is his apple.
2. Those are her pens.
3. That is my ring.
4. These are our keys.
5. That is his brother.
6. These are my pencils.

8.5 🔊
"s" PLURALS:
1. apples 2. bottles 3. necklaces
"es" PLURALS:
4. sandwiches 5. brushes 6. watches
"ies" PLURALS:
7. dictionaries 8. diaries

8.6 🔊
1. watches
2. books
3. sandwiches
4. toothbrushes
5. necklaces
6. apples
7. keys
8. cell phones

8.9
1. This is her laptop. This laptop is hers.
2. Those are their keys. Those keys are theirs.
3. These are our passports. These passports are ours.
4. That is his brush. That brush is his.

8.10
TOM'S BAG:
sandwiches, cell phone, ID card, chocolate bar.
SARAH'S BAG:
purse, books, brush, notebook.

8.11 🔊
1. Those are my books.
2. Those are my dogs.
3. That is my brother.
4. These are my books.
5. These are my dogs.
6. This is my brother.
7. Those are Bruno's books.
8. Those are Bruno's dogs.
9. That is Bruno's brother.
10. These are Bruno's books.
11. These are Bruno's dogs.
12. This is Bruno's brother.

10

10.2 🔊
1. You **are a** doctor.
2. She **is a** farmer.
3. They **are** teachers.
4. We **are** nurses.
5. I **am an** actor.
6. She **is a** chef.

10.3 🔊
1. You **are** a driver.
2. I **am** a mechanic.
3. He **is** a vet.
4. We **are** sales assistants.
5. They **are** businesswomen.
6. She **is** a waitress.
7. We **are** receptionists.
8. She **is** a gardener.

10.5 🔊
1. hospital
2. farm
3. laboratory
4. restaurant
5. school
6. construction site
7. hospital
8. theater
9. restaurant

10.7
1. False 2. False 3. True 4. True

10.9
A. 3
B. 4
C. 1
D. 6
E. 5
F. 2

10.10 🔊
1. She **is a builder. She works on a construction site.**
2. We **are scientists. We work in a laboratory.**
3. You **are an actor. You work in a theater.**
4. He **is a waiter. He works in a restaurant.**
5. Chloe **is a nurse. She works in a hospital.**

10.13
1. Noah's mother
2. Noah's sister
3. Noah's father
4. Noah's brother

10.14 🔊
1. Selma **is a** chef. **She works with** food.
2. Max **is a** nurse. **He works with** patients.
3. Mat **is a** mechanic. **He works with** cars.
4. Ana **is a** vet. **She works with** animals.
5. Jazmin **is a** judge. **She works with** people.

11

11.3 🔊
1. It's midnight.
2. It's half past three.
3. It's quarter to twelve.
4. It's two thirty.
5. It's a quarter past nine.
6. It's ten thirty.

11.4
1. 11:30
2. 7:00
3. 4:15
4. 9:30
5. 2:15

11.5 🔊
1. 9:00
2. 1:15
3. 3:25
4. 2:30
5. 12:15

11.6 🔊
1. It's half past five. / It's five thirty.
2. It's a quarter to seven. / It's six forty-five.
3. It's twenty-five to twelve. / It's eleven thirty-five.
4. It's a quarter past eight. / It's eight fifteen.
5. It's twenty-two past ten. / It's ten twenty-two.

13

13.4 🔊
1. He **wakes** up at 7 o'clock.
2. You **leave** home at 8:30am.
3. I **start** work at 10am.
4. Ellen **gets** up at 5 o'clock.
5. My wife **takes** a shower in the evening.
6. I **take** a shower in the morning.
7. My parents **eat** lunch at 2pm.
8. We **leave** work at 4pm.
9. My brother **works** with animals.

13.5 🔊
1. I **leave** work at 5:30pm.
2. Phil **eats** lunch at 12:30pm.
3. We **get** up at 8am.
4. His son **starts** work at 5am.
5. My sister **leaves** work at 7pm.
6. They **eat** dinner at 10pm.

13.6 🔊
1. My son **wakes** up at 5am.
2. I **leave** work at 6:30pm.
3. We **eat** breakfast at 8am.
4. Paula **works** outside.
5. My wife **starts** work at 7am.
6. He **eats** lunch at noon.

13.9 🔊
1. washes
2. watches
3. wakes
4. goes
5. finishes
6. leaves

13.10 🔊
1. Lucia **wakes** up at 7am.
2. I **get** up at 7:30am.
3. Ethan **goes** to work at 5am.
4. You **leave** work at 5pm.
5. Shona **watches** TV in the evening.

13.11 🔊
1. My mother **watches** TV in the morning.
2. We **go** to bed at midnight.
3. My husband **finishes** work at 6:30pm.
4. Rob **goes** to work at 8:30am.
5. I **take** a shower in the morning.
6. I **leave** work at 6 o'clock in the evening.

13.12
1. True
2. True
3. False
4. False
5. True
6. True

13.13 🔊
1. I start work at noon.
2. I finish work at noon.
3. My brother starts work at noon.
4. My brother finishes work at noon.
5. They start work at noon.
6. They finish work at noon.
7. I start work at 2:30pm.
8. I finish work at 2:30pm.
9. My brother starts work at 2:30pm.
10. My brother finishes work at 2:30pm.
11. They start work at 2:30pm.
12. They finish work at 2:30pm.

14

14.3 🔊
1. We eat lunch at 3pm **on** the weekend / **at** the weekend.
2. She goes to bed at 1am **on** the weekend / **at** the weekend.
3. I go to work **from** Monday **to** Wednesday.
4. They eat dinner at 9pm **on** the weekend / **at** the weekend.
5. We finish work at 3pm **on** Fridays.
6. I eat breakfast at work **on** Mondays.

14.5 🔊
1. He **goes to the gym** on Tuesdays and Fridays.
2. They **go swimming** on Thursdays.
3. He **plays soccer** on Wednesdays.
4. I **take a bath** on the weekend.
5. You **read the newspaper** on Saturdays.

14.6 🔊
1. I watch TV **on** Sundays.
2. I take a bath **at** 7pm every day.
3. I go to bed **at** 10 o'clock **on** Sundays.
4. I get up **at** 8am **from** Monday to Friday.

14.10
1. True 2. True 3. False 4. True
5. False

14.11 🔊
1. I get up at 6am five days a week.
2. They go to bed at 11pm every day.
3. Sarah plays soccer twice a week.
4. Jamie washes his clothes once a week.

14.12 🔊
1. We get up **at** 7am five times a week
2. They go to work **from** Monday to Friday.
3. Linda washes her face **every** day.
4. Colin sleeps **from** 11pm **to** 6am.

15

15.4 🔊
1. She is not my sister.
2. That is not her car.
3. I am not 35 years old.
4. We are not Spanish.
5. Chad is not a vet.

15.5 🔊
1. He **is not** in the office.
2. She **is not** a businesswoman.
3. I **am not** 18 years old.
4. This **is not** a snake.
5. We **are not** artists.
6. You **are not** at work.
7. Dexter **is not** a cat.

15.6
A. 3
B. 1
C. 5
D. 2
E. 4

15.9 🔊
1. It **is not** 10 o'clock in the morning.
2. You **aren't** 35 years old.
3. I **am not** Australian.
4. My brother **isn't** married.
5. Tom and Angela **aren't** construction workers.

15.10
1. True
2. True
3. False
4. True
5. False
6. True
7. False

15.11 🔊
1. I am not at work.
2. I am not tired.
3. I am not 24 years old.
4. You aren't at work.
5. You aren't tired.
6. You aren't 24 years old.

7. He isn't at work.
8. He isn't tired.
9. He isn't 24 years old.
10. They aren't at work.
11. They aren't tired.
12. They aren't 24 years old.

16

16.4 ◀))
1. I **do not** read the papers on Saturday.
2. The dog **does not** eat fish.
3. They **do not** go to the theater often.
4. Ben and I **do not** live on a farm now.
5. Theo **does not** cycle to work.
6. You **do not** work at Fabio's café.
7. Claire **does not** watch TV in the evening.
8. We **do not** play football at home.
9. Pierre **does not** wake up before noon.

16.5
1. False
2. True
3. False
4. False

16.8
1. We go to work every day. We do not go to work every day.
2. He watches TV in the evening. He doesn't watch TV in the evening.
3. You do not work in an office. You don't work in an office.
4. They play tennis. They do not play tennis.
5. She works with children. She doesn't work with children.

16.9 ◀))
1. We don't work with animals.
2. I don't eat chocolate.
3. Sandy doesn't work in a hairdresser's.
4. Melanie and Cris don't have a car.
5. They don't live in Park Road now.
6. We don't watch Hollywood movies.
7. She doesn't drive a taxi.

16.10 ◀))
1. I don't work outside.
2. I don't have a bicycle.
3. I don't play tennis.
4. You don't work outside.
5. You don't have a bicycle.
6. You don't play tennis.
7. We don't work outside.
8. We don't have a bicycle.
9. We don't play tennis.
10. Meg doesn't work outside.
11. Meg doesn't have a bicycle.
12. Meg doesn't play tennis.

16.11
1. Kim
2. Selma
3. Chiyo
4. Maria
5. Selma

17

17.4 ◀))
1. Is Brad a nurse?
2. Are these my keys?
3. Are Ruby and Farid actors?
4. Is this his laptop?
5. Is Valeria his sister?

17.5
1. A
2. B
3. B
4. A
5. A
6. B

17.7 ◀))
1. **Is** Holly your mother?
2. **Are** they from Argentina?
3. **Are** you a teacher?
4. **Is** this your dog?
5. **Is** there a post office?

17.11 ◀))
1. **Do** you get up at 7am?
2. **Do** they live at number 59?
3. **Do** we finish work at 6pm today?
4. **Does** the parrot talk all day?
5. **Do** you work in a lab?

17.12 ◀))
1. Do you live in New York?
2. Does she work on a farm?
3. Does he get up at 5am every day?
4. Do they come from Peru?
5. Does Brad work in the post office?

17.13 ◀))
1. Do they live in New York City?
2. Does he work in a restaurant?
3. Does Lewis go swimming on Fridays?
4. Does Marisha work with animals?

17.14 ◀))
1. **Does** she go swimming on Tuesdays?
2. **Do** you read the paper on Sundays?
3. **Does** she work with animals?
4. **Do** they work on a construction site?

18

18.3
1. True
2. False
3. False
4. True
5. False

18.4 ◀))
1. No, it isn't.
2. Yes, it is.
3. Yes, she does.
4. No, I don't.
5. No, it isn't.

18.5 ◀))
1. No, **I'm not**
2. Yes, **they do.**
3. No, **it isn't.**
4. Yes, **she does.**
5. No, **she isn't.**
6. Yes, **they do.**
7. No, **he isn't.**

19

19.3 ◀))
1. What **are** their names?
2. What **is** the time?
3. What **are** my favorite colors?
4. What **is** the hotel next to?
5. What **are** they?
6. What **is** your uncle's name?
7. What **is** my name?

19.6 ◀))
1. What is the time? It's 5 o'clock.
2. When is your birthday? July 23.
3. Which is your car? The red Ferrari.
4. Why are you here? For a meeting.
5. How old are you? I'm 25.
6. Who is there? It's me, Marcus.

19.7 ◀))
1. **Where** are your parents from?
2. **How** old are you?
3. **When** is breakfast?
4. **Who** is your friend talking to?
5. **Why** is it cold in here?
6. **Which** person is your teacher?

19.11 ◀))
1. When **does** she eat lunch?
2. Where **do** they live?
3. Which bag **do** you want?
4. Where **does** he come from?
5. When **does** the movie end?

19.12 🔊
1. Where does he play football?
2. When do you clean the car?
3. What time does the party start?
4. Which days do you play tennis?

19.13
1. When do you eat breakfast?
2. What do you study?
3. Where do you work?
4. Who is she?

19.14 🔊
1. **Where** do you work in the city?
2. **When** do you start work?
3. **What** time does it open?
4. **How** many people do you work with?
5. **Who** do you work with?

19.15
1. Her brother
2. Two
3. 7am
4. Goes swimming
5. By the pool
6. Tomorrow

19.16 🔊
1. Where does Kate play golf?
2. Where do they play golf?
3. Where do you play golf?
4. Where does Kate go to the gym?
5. Where do they go to the gym?
6. Where do you go to the gym?
7. When does Kate play golf?
8. When do they play golf?
9. When do you play golf?
10. When does Kate go to the gym?
11. When do they go to the gym?
12. When do you go to the gym?

19.17 🔊
1. How often **do** they play tennis?
2. Which office **does** he work in?
3. Where **is** the party?
4. What **do** you do?

19.18 🔊
1. What **is her cat called**?
2. Who **is your English teacher**?
3. Where **does Ben work**?
4. How **is your grandmother**?

21

21.3 🔊
1. **There are** two churches.
2. **There is** a swimming pool.
3. **There is** a library.
4. **There are** two castles.

21.4
1. airports
2. theaters
3. schools
4. hospitals
5. bars
6. churches
7. factories
8. offices

21.5 🔊
1. There are two schools.
2. There are two cafés.
3. There is a hospital.
4. There is a restaurant.
5. There are three stores.

21.7 🔊
1. There **isn't** a theater.
2. There **aren't** any factories.
3. There **isn't** a bus station.
4. There **aren't** any airports.
5. There **aren't** any churches.

21.10 🔊
1. There **are** no castles.
2. There **aren't** any factories.
3. There **are** no hospitals.
4. There **aren't** any churches.
5. There **are** no swimming pools.
6. There **are** no airports.

21.11
A. 3
B. 1
C. 2
D. 4

21.12
1. True
2. False
3. False
4. True

21.13 🔊
1. **There isn't** a park.
2. **There is** a hotel.
3. **There are** no cafés.
4. **There isn't** an airport.
5. **There are** two stores.
6. **There isn't** a train station.
7. **There are** two theaters.

22

22.3 🔊
1. **The** new teacher is called Miss Jones.
2. There is **a** good café in the park.
3. I work at **the** hotel next to the library.
4. There is **a** swimming pool near my office.
5. It is **the** dog's favorite toy.

6. Janie is **an** artist at the gallery.
7. See you at **the** café at the bus station.

22.6 🔊
1. There are **some** stores on Broad Street.
2. There is **a** café next to the castle.
3. There are **some** cakes on the table.
4. There is **a** phone here.
5. There are **some** factories downtown.

22.7 🔊
1. There **are** some supermarkets in town.
2. There **is** an office near the river.
3. There **are** some chocolate bars in my bag.
4. There **is** a hospital near the bus station.

22.10 🔊
1. Are there **any** stores on your street?
2. Is there **an** airport near Littleton?
3. Are there **any** mosques in the city?
4. Is there **a** swimming pool downtown?
5. Are there **any** offices in that building?

22.11 🔊
1. Is there a supermarket near here?
2. Are there any cafés on Elm Road?
3. Are there any hotels near your house?
4. Is there a café near your office?
5. Is there a bar next to the bank?

22.13 🔊
1. Yes, **there is**.
2. Yes, **there are**.
3. No, **there isn't**.
4. Yes, **there are**.
5. No, **there isn't**.
6. No, **there aren't**.

22.14 🔊
1. Yes, there are.
2. No, there isn't.
3. No, there aren't.
4. Yes, there is.

23

23.3 🔊
1. Wake up
2. Do
3. Start
4. Have
5. Wait
6. Stop
7. Work

23.5 🔊
1. Take the second right. The station is on left.
2. Take the first left, then turn right. The restaurant is on the right.
3. Take the second left, and the hospital is on the right.

4 Take the first left, then go straight ahead. The hotel is on the right.
5 Take the first left, then turn left. The castle is on the right.

23.7 ◄»)
1 The supermarket is **next to** the post office.
2 The museum is **behind** the café.
3 The station is **in front of** the church.
4 The cinema is on the **corner** of the intersection.
5 The post office is **between** the café and the supermarket.

23.10 ◄»)
1 Don't read that book.
2 Don't go past the hotel.
3 Don't give that to the cat.
4 Don't have a shower.
5 Don't drive to the mall.

23.11
1 Library
2 Swimming pool
3 Movie theater
4 Science museum

24

24.3 ◄»)
1 There are two hotels and three shops.
2 Hilda works in a school and a theater.
3 My uncle is a scientist and my aunt is a doctor.
4 Sue watches TV and she reads books.
5 The store opens at night and Jan starts work.

24.4
A 3
C 1
D 4
E 2

24.6 ◄»)
1 There are hotels, bars, and stores.
2 Sam eats breakfast, lunch, and dinner.
3 I play tennis, soccer, and chess.
4 Teo plays with his car, train, and bus.
5 There is a pencil, a bag, and a cell phone.
6 My friends, girlfriend, and aunt are here.
7 Ling works on Monday, Thursday, and Friday.

24.8 ◄»)
1 This is my car, but these aren't my car keys.
2 We eat a small breakfast, but we eat a big lunch.
3 I work from Monday to Friday, but not on the weekend.
4 The bathroom has a shower, but it doesn't have a bathtub.

24.9 ◄»)
1 There isn't a bathtub, but there is a shower.
2 There isn't a bar, but there is a café.
3 The bag is Maya's, but that laptop isn't hers.
4 Si doesn't have any dogs, but he has two cats.
5 Sally reads books, but she never watches TV.

24.10 ◄»)
1 Lu reads books **and** magazines.
2 I work every weekday, **but** not on weekends.
3 Jim is a husband **and** a father.
4 There is a cinema, **but** no theater.
5 There isn't a gym, **but** there is a pool.

24.11 ◄»)
1 There is a cat and a rabbit, but there isn't a snake.
2 There is a doctor and a builder, but not a chef.
3 There is a laptop and a newspaper, but there isn't a cell phone.
4 There is a movie theater and a restaurant, but not a theater.

25

25.3 ◄»)
1 He is a horrible man.
2 They are small children.
3 My uncle is a quiet man.
4 There is a large cake.
5 These are my old shoes.
6 There is a new supermarket.
7 You work in an old museum.

25.5
1. **small** 2. **beautiful** 3. **old** 4. **large** 5. **busy**
6. **horrible** 7. **beautiful**

25.6
1 The nurse is busy. She is busy.
2 The dog is quiet. It is quiet.
3 The patients are new. They are new.
4 The town is horrible. It is horrible.
5 The car is beautiful. It is beautiful.

25.8
1 beautiful
2 lake
3 large
4 mountains
5 restaurant
6 beach
7 busy
8 quiet

25.9 ◄»)
1 **The** countryside **is** quiet **and the** trees **are** beautiful.
2 **The** city **is** horrible **and the** people **are** busy.
3 **The** hotel **is** new **and the** swimming pool **is** large.

4 **The** beach **is** big **and the** cafés **are** busy.
5 **The** city **is** old **and the** buildings **are** beautiful.

25.12
A 2
B 5
C 1
D 4
E 3
F 6

25.13 ◄»)
1 There are **lots of** people.
2 There are **some** buildings.
3 There are **a few** cars.
4 There are **a few** parks.

25.14 ◄»)
1 In the tree, there are a few birds and some apples.
2 In the sea, there are a few people and lots of fish.
3 In the countryside, there are some people and lots of trees.

26

26.3
1 lives there.
2 she's a farmer.
3 goes swimming.
4 it's new.
5 with people.
6 her aunt lives there.
7 lots of people.

26.4 ◄»)
1 She lives on a farm because **she's a farmer**.
2 She works in a hotel because **she's a receptionist**.
3 They get up late because **they're students**.
4 We work with children because **we're teachers**.
5 You don't eat lunch because **you're busy**.
6 I work outside because **I'm a gardener**.
7 My parents go to the country because **it's quiet**.

28

28.3 ◄»)
1 They **have** a car.
2 You **have** a chair.
3 He **has** a dog.
4 We **have** a daughter.
5 It **has** a door.

28.4
1 Maya **2** Ben **3** Ben **4** Ben

28.5

1. False
2. True
3. False
4. False
5. True
6. True

28.7 🔊

1. Kaleh does not have a dog.
2. You don't have a microwave.
3. Greendale does not have a church.
4. Alyssa and Logan don't have a garage.
5. We do not have a yard.

28.8 🔊

1. I have a couch.
2. I have some chairs.
3. I have a dining room.
4. We have a couch.
5. We have some chairs.
6. We have a dining room.
7. She has a couch.
8. She has some chairs.
9. She has a dining room.
10. She doesn't have a couch.
11. She doesn't have a dining room.

28.11

1. They have not got a couch. They haven't got a couch.
2. He has got three sisters. He's got three sisters.
3. You have not got a bike. You haven't got a bike.
4. We have got a microwave. We've got a microwave.
5. It has got a bathtub. It's got a bathtub.
6. They have got a cat. They've got a cat.

29

29.3 🔊

1. Do they have a toaster?
2. Do you have a new couch?
3. Does Ben have a washing machine?
4. Do we have an old armchair?
5. Does Karen have a large TV?
6. Does the kitchen have a sink?
7. Does the house have a yard?

29.4

1. Lucy
2. Lucy
3. Lucy
4. Tim
5. Tim

29.5 🔊

1. Do you have any chairs?
2. Do you have a kettle?
3. Do you have any plates?
4. Do they have any chairs?

5. Do they have a kettle?
6. Do they have any plates?
7. Does he have any chairs?
8. Does he have a kettle?
9. Does he have any plates?

29.7 🔊

1. No, I don't.
2. Yes, I do.
3. Yes, I do.
4. No, I don't.

29.8 🔊

1. No, he doesn't.
2. No, he doesn't.
3. Yes, he does.

29.10 🔊

1. Has this town got a theater?
2. Has your house got an attic?
3. Have they got laptops?
4. Has this coffee shop got a bathroom?
5. Have you got a cell phone?
6. Has the teacher got my book?

29.11 🔊

1. Yes, **she has.**
2. Yes, **it has.**
3. No, **they haven't.**
4. No, **it hasn't.**

31

31.3 🔊

1. Jake has **an** apple.
2. There is **some** coffee.
3. Reena eats **some** spaghetti.
4. There are **some** eggs.
5. I've got **some** bananas.

31.5

1. There is some milk. There isn't any milk.
2. Is there any chocolate? There isn't any chocolate.
3. Are there any apples? There are some apples.

31.6 🔊

1. Yes, **there is.**
2. No, **there aren't.**
3. No, **there isn't.**

31.9 🔊

1. There is **a bag of** flour.
2. There is **a cup of** coffee.
3. There is **a carton of** juice.
4. There are **two bowls of** spaghetti.
5. There are **two glasses of** milk.

31.12 🔊

1. **How many** glasses of juice are there?
2. **How much** water is there?
3. **How many** potatoes are there?
4. **How many** bars of chocolate are there?
5. **How much** pasta is there?
6. **How many** cartons of juice are there?
7. **How much** milk is there?

31.13

1. one bag
2. three
3. some
4. cheese

32

32.3 🔊

1. There are **enough** oranges.
2. You have **enough** pineapples.
3. There are **too many** apples.
4. You don't have **enough** bananas.

32.6

1. Too many
2. Not enough
3. Enough
4. Too much

32.7 🔊

1. There is **too much** sugar.
2. They **don't have** enough butter.
3. She has **too many** mangoes.
4. John has too many **eggs.**
5. There **aren't** enough oranges.
6. That **is too much** flour.
7. There **is** too much sugar in the cake.

34

34.2 🔊

1. Hannah **chooses** a yellow skirt.
2. Elliot and Ruby **buy** a new couch.
3. Sue **owns** an old winter coat.
4. Jess's dad **buys** her a new bike.
5. Chris and Lisa **own** a black sports car.
6. Gayle and Mike **sell** shoes at the market.
7. Mia **chooses** her red shoes.
8. The shoes **fit** me.
9. We **want** new white shirts.

34.3 🔊

1. They choose expensive blue sweaters.
2. Judith has some old brown hats.
3. This shop sells short red pants.
4. Tina owns cheap black shoes.
5. Jim buys a new black coat.

34.4

1. **new** 2. **cheap** 3. **white** 4. **long** 5. **black**
6. **black** 7. **old** 8. **new** 9. **expensive** 10. **cheap**
11. **red** 12. **long**

34.5

1. a blue hat
2. a new t-shirt
3. a cheap skirt
4. a black coat

34.7

1. too cheap
2. too expensive
3. too long
4. too short
5. too old
6. too new
7. too big

34.8 ◀))

1. Jim's pants are **too short**.
2. Sam's dress is **too long**.
3. Molly's sweater is **too small**.
4. Helen's red hat is **too big**.
5. Lili's shoes are **too big**.

34.9

1. B
2. A
3. B
4. A
5. A

34.10 ◀))

1. These black pants are too big.
2. These black pants are big enough.
3. These black pants are too short.
4. My expensive pants are too big.
5. My expensive pants are big enough.
6. My expensive pants are too short.
7. My black dress is too big.
8. My black dress is big enough.
9. My black dress is too short.
10. My expensive dress is too big.
11. My expensive dress is big enough.
12. My expensive dress is too short.

35

35.4 ◀))

1. This is a **horrible** old t-shirt.
2. This is a **boring** movie.
3. I have a **lovely** long dress.
4. This is a **beautiful** bird.
5. This is a **fun** party.

35.5 ◀))

1. That is a horrible blue car.
2. This is a fun short story.
3. I have a lovely black cat.

4. He has an ugly red house.
5. They own a great new laptop.

35.6

1. A
2. B
3. A
4. A

35.8 ◀))

1. Oh, no, the blue glass vase!
2. We have two plastic chairs.
3. What an interesting metal box!
4. That's an expensive leather couch.

35.9 ◀))

1. She owns some beautiful wooden chairs.
2. We don't own those horrible
plastic plates.
3. They have an ugly yellow car.
4. He wears a boring blue sweater.
5. She wants a new metal lamp.
6. He owns a large fabric bag.
7. Norah wants a new leather jacket.

37

37.3 ◀))

1. We don't **go surfing** in the winter.
2. Do you **go sailing** on the weekend?
3. Tipo **goes cycling** five times a week.
4. He **goes fishing** on the river.
5. Sharon **goes dancing** with her friend.
6. Do they **go running** every morning?
7. He doesn't **go horse riding**.

37.4

1. salsa dancing
2. fishing
3. cycling
4. surfing

37.6 ◀))

REGULAR GERUNDS:
sailing, **snowboarding**, **skateboarding**
GERUNDS WITH DOUBLE CONSONANTS:
swimming, **running**, **shopping**
GERUNDS WITH A DROPPED "E":
skating, **horse riding**, **cycling**

37.9 ◀))

1. Shala **doesn't play** tennis.
2. Mina **plays** golf at the club.
3. We **play** squash on Mondays.
4. The dog **plays** with its ball.
5. Maria **doesn't play** tennis.
6. The kids **don't play** games at school.
7. They **play** soccer at the park.

37.10 ◀))

1. We **play** tennis every Tuesday night.
2. They **don't play** golf during the week.
3. You **don't play** volleyball at the beach.
4. Do they **play** together every Saturday?

37.11

1. Sara
2. Chas
3. Sara
4. Cassie

37.12 ◀))

1. Milo and I **go cycling** in the park
on Saturdays.
2. The team **plays /play football** from 6pm
to 7pm on Wednesdays.
3. Imelda **goes horse riding** once a month.
4. Luther **goes fishing** during his vacation time.
5. Hannah **plays tennis** with her cousin
on Monday evenings.

39

39.3 ◀))

1. We never go to the mall.
2. Sally and Ken usually cycle to work.
3. My sister often works outside.

39.4

1. usually
2. never
3. usually
4. often
5. always

39.5 ◀))

1. Nico **usually** swims after work. He **never**
watches TV on the weekend.
2. Meg **often** goes surfing in Hawaii. She
sometimes dances all night.
3. Alma **always** reads on vacation. She
sometimes plays golf on Sundays.
4. Carrie **usually** goes to bed late and she **never**
eats breakfast.

39.8 ◀))

1. How often do they go to work?
2. When do you get up?
3. How often do you go on vacation?
4. When do they go shopping?
5. How often do you visit Mischa?

39.9 ◀))

1. When do they visit their grandparents?
2. When do we go skating?
3. How often does he play hockey?
4. When do you go shopping?
5. How often do they see their parents?
6. How often does he walk the dog?
7. How often do we go skating on the lake?

39.10 🔊

1. When do you do yoga?
2. How often do you go to the movies?
3. How often do you go skateboarding?
4. When do you arrive at work?
5. How often do you go surfing?

40

40.3 🔊

1. Ava and Elsa love the mountains.
2. Shania hates mice.
3. Manuel loves his book.
4. Cats don't like the rain.

40.4

1. Imelda doesn't hate pasta.
2. My dog doesn't love steak.
3. Our grandfather doesn't like coffee.
4. I don't love the sea.
5. Sam and Jen don't hate hockey.
6. You don't like the countryside.
7. We don't like our new cell phones.

40.5

1. hockey
2. some actors
3. pizza
4. spiders

40.6 🔊

1. I love cats.
2. I love curry.
3. I love this house.
4. You love cats.
5. You love curry.
6. You love this house.
7. Milly hates cats.
8. Milly hates curry.
9. Milly hates this house.

40.9

1. D
2. B
3. C
4. A

40.10

1. True
2. False
3. False
4. True
5. False
6. True
7. False
8. True
9. True

40.14 🔊

1. Why does Una love skiing?
2. Why do they like this book?
3. Why doesn't Debbie like her job?
4. Do we like cooking?
5. Does she love surfing?
6. Do I hate working late?
7. Does Aziz love Ontario?

40.15 🔊

1. I like English class because it's interesting.
2. We love skating because it's exciting.
3. He hates cleaning because it's boring.

42

42.3

1. basketball
2. fish
3. Rome
4. gardener
5. Italian
6. running
7. cooking

42.4

1. A
2. B
3. A
4. C
5. A

42.5 🔊

1. Grace's favorite food is pizza.
2. Poppy's favorite sport is surfing.
3. Dylan's favorite animal is his horse.
4. Justin's favorite country is Australia.
5. Ling's favorite pastime is knitting.
6. Abdul's favorite color is purple.
7. Mira's favorite number is 10.
8. Jacob's favorite sweater is woolen.
9. Tori's favorite relative is her cousin.

42.6 🔊

1. Sam's **favorite band** is Big Bang.
2. Joe's favorite band is **Fun Sounds**.
3. Joni's **favorite restaurant** is Midnight Pizza.
4. Sam's favorite restaurant is **The Salad Bar**.
5. Joe's **favorite resaurant** is Burger Heaven.
6. Joni **loves the play** called Big Blue Sea.
7. Joe loves the movie called **Blue Soul**.

42.7

1. yoga
2. burgers
3. surfing
4. eating dinner in a restaurant

44

44.4 🔊

1. Paul cannot ride a bicycle.
2. Manuel cannot come to the party.
3. They can sleep in the tent tonight.
4. I cannot walk up the hill.
5. I can carry this box to the car.

44.5 🔊

1. Jo's pen doesn't work. She **can't** write her letter.
2. I understand the homework, so I **can** do it.
3. The museum is closed. We **can't** get in.
4. I have car today, so I **can** drive you.
5. It's cold outside, so we **can't** have a picnic.
6. Tony needs to work late, so he **can't** come.
7. We **can't** play tennis. It's too dark.

44.6

1. Shirley can drive a car. Shirley can't drive a car.
2. Ben and Julie cannot carry boxes. Ben and Julie can't carry boxes.
3. Ilaria can spell English words. Ilaria cannot spell English words.
4. He can go to work. He can't go to work.

44.9 🔊

1. No, **he can't.**
2. Yes, **they can.**
3. No, **I can't.**
4. Yes, **I can.**
5. No, **we can't.**
6. Yes, **she can.**
7. No, **they can't.**

44.10 🔊

1. Can the dog jump over the wall?
2. Can Denise touch her toes?
3. Can I lift my son onto my shoulders?
4. Can Grandma see the TV?
5. Can I hit the tennis ball over the net?

44.11

1. True
2. False
3. True
4. True

44.12 🔊

1. Paul and Jerry don't like the ocean because they **cannot** swim.
2. I ride my bike to work because I **cannot** drive.
3. Jim cannot climb over the wall, but he **can** walk around it.
4. My mother **cannot** lift that bag because it's too heavy.
5. My sister Penny loves music and can dance to any song.

45.3 ◀))
1. Mary can speak French **excellently**.
2. Roger can run very **quickly**.
3. The old man walks **slowly**.
4. He talks very **loudly**.
5. She won the race **easily**.

45.5
REGULAR
loudly, quickly, badly, easily
IRREGULAR
fast, well, hard, early

45.6 ◀))
1. You speak English very **well**.
2. Damian cooks burgers **badly**.
3. I can get to your house **easily**.
4. Benjy always listens **carefully**.
5. My brother always works **hard**.
6. Sammy always plays his guitar **loudly**.

45.10 ◀))
1. My horse is good at jumping.
2. I am bad at getting up early.
3. Mary is bad at writing German.
4. Jo and Bob are good at swimming.
5. Millie is bad at cleaning.

45.11 ◀))
1. Conchita is good at playing basketball.
2. You can drive a van well.
3. Shania and Dave are good at surfing.
4. My father can't speak English well.
5. Manu is bad at writing stories.

45.12
1. Bad at
2. Bad at
3. Bad at
4. Good at

45.13 ◀))
1. I am good at cooking.
2. I am bad at cooking.
3. I am good at playing soccer.
4. I am bad at playing soccer.
5. I am good at history.
6. I am bad at history.
7. He is good at cooking.
8. He is bad at cooking.
9. He is good at playing soccer.
10. He is bad at playing soccer.
11. He is good at history.
12. He is bad at history.

46.3 ◀))
1. A tortoise walks very slowly.
2. A chicken flies quite badly.
3. Pigs eat very noisily.
4. Monkeys climb trees really well.

46.5
1. Really good
2. Quite good
3. Quite good
4. Really good

47.4
1. I want to get a dog.
I would like to get a dog.
2. You want to work in Turkey.
You'd like to work in Turkey.
3. We would like to learn Chinese.
We'd like to learn Chinese.
4. They want to start a rock band.
They would like to start a rock band.

47.5 ◀))
1. He'd like to act in a musical.
2. He wants to be in the Olympics.
3. He'd like to travel around Asia.
4. She'd like to sail a boat.
5. She wants to work with lions in Africa.

47.6 ◀))
1. I'd like to climb this tree.
2. I'd like to climb that mountain.
3. I'd like to read a newspaper.
4. I'd like to read another book.
5. I want to climb this tree.
6. I want to climb that mountain.
7. I want to read a newspaper.
8. I want to read another book.
9. She wants to climb this tree.
10. She wants to climb that mountain.
11. She wants to read a newspaper.
12. She wants to read another book.

47.9
1. He would not like to play tennis.
He wouldn't like to play tennis.
2. She would not like to study science.
She doesn't want to study science.
3. They would not like to go to work.
They wouldn't like to go to work.
4. You wouldn't like to sing tonight.
You don't want to sing tonight.

5. We would not like to go diving.
We don't want to go diving.

47.11
1. No, she wouldn't.
2. Yes, he does.
3. Yes, he would.
4. No, she doesn't.
5. Yes, she would.

47.12 ◀))
1. He doesn't want to climb that hill.
2. I wouldn't like to be a judge.
3. They don't want to go to work today.
4. She would like to play tennis tonight.
5. I want to climb that tree.

48.5 ◀))
1. Jerry would really like to pass his driving test.
2. Ben and Sam would really like to take an IELTS test.
3. Helen would quite like to practice her English.
4. I'd quite like to play the piano tonight.

48.6 ◀))
1. I'd really like to practice my spelling.
2. I'd really like to do a biology degree.
3. I'd really like to learn English.
4. I'd quite like to practice my spelling.
5. I'd quite like to do a biology degree.
6. I'd quite like to learn English.
7. Laila would really like to pass her history exam.
8. Laila would really like to do a biology degree.
9. Laila would really like to learn English.
10. Laila would quite like to pass her history exam.
11. Laila would quite like to do a biology degree.
12. Laila would quite like to learn English.

48.9 ◀))
1. Emily has **a lovely home**.
2. Sue always takes her lunch to **the office**.
3. Can you see where **the church** is?
4. Jim went to **bed** hours ago.
5. Can you drive me into **town** later?
6. I live next to **the university**.
7. I leave **home** at 8am every weekday.

48.10
1. Tom
2. Frank
3. Sophie
4. Charlie
5. Sarah.

Index

All entries are indexed by unit number.
Main entries are highlighted in **bold**.

Acknowledgments

The publisher would like to thank:
Jo Kent, Trish Burrow, and Emma Watkins for additional text; Thomas Booth, Helen Fanthorpe, Helen Leech, Carrie Lewis, and Vicky Richards for editorial assistance; Stephen Bere, Sarah Hilder, Amy Child, Fiona Macdonald, and Simon Murrell for additional design work; Simon Mumford for maps and national flags; Peter Chrisp for fact checking; Penny Hands, Amanda Learmonth, and Carrie Lewis for proofreading; Elizabeth Wise for indexing; Tatiana Boyko, Rory Farrell, Clare Joyce, and Viola Wang for additional illustrations; Liz Hammond for editing audio scripts and managing audio recordings; Hannah Bowen and Scarlett O'Hara for compiling audio scripts; George Flamouridis for mixing and mastering audio recordings; Heather Hughes, Tommy Callan, Tom Morse, Gillian Reid, and Sonia Charbonnier for creative technical support; Vishal Bhatia, Kartik Gera, Sachin Gupta, Shipra Jain, Deepak Mittal, Nehal Verma, Roohi Rais, Jaileen Kaur, Anita Yadav, Manish Upreti, Nisha Shaw, Ankita Yadav, and Priyanka Kharbanda for technical assistance.

All images are copyright DK.
For more information, please visit
www.dkimages.com.